THE DOOMSDAY JOB
the behavioral anatomy of turnover

Other books by Dean B. Peskin
THE ART OF JOB HUNTING
THE BUILDING BLOCKS OF EEO
HUMAN BEHAVIOR AND
EMPLOYMENT INTERVIEWING

THE DOOMSDAY JOB

the behavioral anatomy of turnover

DEAN B. PESKIN

A Division of American Management Associations

© 1973 AMACOM
A division of American Management Associations, Inc., New York.
All rights reserved. Printed in the United States of America.

This publication may not be reproduced, stored in a retrieval system,
or transmitted in whole or in part, in any form or by any means,
electronic, mechanical, photocopying, recording, or otherwise,
without the prior written permission of AMACOM.

International standard book number: 0-8144-5310-4
Library of Congress catalog card number: 72-84118

First printing

to Marcia
a steadfast companion who never faltered when the going was rough

preface
probe the present

DOOMSDAY JOBS exist in all organizations and at all levels, causing disillusionment and stifling human energies. The long-range curse for business is the inability to meet tomorrow's management challenge: change. The immediate results are turnover and lost profits.

The words *turnover* and *lost profits* have more impact than *change* because they represent a more immediate threat. Change too is threatening, but it appears less immediate, perhaps even avoidable. It is not, of course. Change will not incubate until all risks are eliminated. It is the avoidance of change and the unwillingness to accommodate risk and inspire innovation that lead to costly turnover and lost profits.

The important changes of the 1970s and beyond are known or conjectured even now. These changes represent real opportunities for business in the areas of profits and public service. The payoffs, and they are high, can be achieved only with a stable and motivated workforce. For those who welcome change, the years ahead will be the "age of wisdom . . . the spring of hope"; for those who fear it, they will be the "age of foolishness . . . the winter of despair."

A generation is rising of involved and altruistic, disgruntled and protesting people who have cut their teeth on "doing their own thing." They are the 15- to 25-year-olds, the fastest-growing age group in America, and their brothers and sisters a decade older. These are the people who defied and successfully delayed the plans of Consolidated Edison of New York to build a nuclear power plant because they wanted to preserve the ecology of the proposed plant site despite the threat of imminent power failure. These are the people who have done more to make racial equality a reality than all the legislative and administrative action to date. These are also the people who challenged Dow Chemical's recruitment on campus, forced Lockheed's annual meeting into a guarded hangar, and protested the firing of a Stanford University professor more loudly than fire bombings of the Bank of America in San Francisco.

They will perhaps take more credit for social, economic, and political changes than historians may be willing to grant. But they have made themselves felt by attracting attention to many real and important issues that have gained popular support. Their behavior has been rewarded by recognition and emulation. They have every reason to continue the behavior that has brought them these rewards. Age may mellow them and make their tactics less theatrical, but their humanistic philosophy is not likely to be diluted. And these are the men and women who will populate not only the marketplace but the business organization.

The emphasis on the human dimension of business is not new, of course. Corporations and their management no longer enjoy favored immunity from labor, government, and consumer pressure. Workers call upon their unions to play ever more vital third-party roles. Government regulations and consumer action aimed at product purity, health protection, equal employment opportunities, fair labor practices, safety on the job, minimum wages, and other areas of special interest force these realities on the business community.

Three fundamental assumptions about the future seem reasonable.

First, man will survive. Natural disasters and his own destructive bents—in the form of war, pollution, overpopulation—will not deny him the future.

Second, man will be a different kind of wanting animal. He will be more concerned about the nature of his environment and the sociopolitical and economic arenas. He will be concerned specifically about the nature of the business enterprise. Contemporary man wants encounters with his own destiny and with contemporary realities. He is no longer content with a passive, pushbutton role or intimidated by the real or imagined coercive power of executive management. And in his work he wants moral choice and intellectual content.

Third, business decentralization will accelerate and become increasingly multidimensional. The business environment will have to encompass socioeconomic and political aspects, making corporate objectives sensitive to internal and external social consequences. Companies once functioned on the concept of an unchanging or slowly evolving environment. Now the environment in which men live and work is rapidly changing. One result is that the search for profits will spread worldwide as traditional markets dwindle.

This shift will propel business into a change of role, from operating solely as a supplier of goods and services to accepting responsibility for satisfying the market demand that it improve the quality of life. This will mean a significant redefinition of business success and profit. And it will mean that the business manager of tomorrow will be as different from the manager of yesterday as a supersonic jet pilot is from the Red Baron. The effective leader must be perceptive, sensitive to human reactions, and clearly people-oriented. The days are over for hard-nosed, tough-as-nails "technologists." They exist but are remnants.

Expanding markets, social relevance for corporate survival, and contribution to the quality of life can be achieved only through a work environment that is self-correcting and technologically renewing. Businesses that create such an environment attract and retain people who believe in their mission, have confidence in their leaders, and gain satisfaction from their occupational experience. The process—organization renewal begetting employee commitment—will defeat the turnover syndrome by eradicating its cause: the doomsday job.

DEAN B. PESKIN

contents

ONE	humanizing the doomsday job	1
TWO	renewing the doomsday organization	19
THREE	technical specialization	33
FOUR	a study of waste: minority employees	49
FIVE	turnover costs can be measured	67
SIX	pinpointing the causes of turnover	79
SEVEN	exit interviews: pros and cons	91
EIGHT	improving the employment process	103
NINE	improving the promotion process	121
TEN	a turnover action program	135
postscript	look to the future	151
index		157

ONE

humanizing
the doomsday job

2 The Doomsday Job

WHAT MAKES a job doomsday? Is it poor work content, a destructive work environment, friction in the interpersonal work relationships? It can be any of these. But behind them all lies a common cause—dehumanizing elements in the organization's culture that ignore or contravene the worker's values and needs.

How effectively a business functions depends critically on how well its people function. The ultimate success of the organization is the result of committed and participating human beings. The employee's performance in turn reflects three conditions that mold every job, whatever its nature:

1. The degree of the employee's internal motivation.
2. The correspondence between the goals of the employee and those of the organization.
3. External forces spurring the employee to action through stimulators such as punishment and reward systems and the frequency, duration, and intensity of these stimulating forces.

When one or more of these conditions is negative, it introduces doom into the job. At its least the doomsday job curtails growth, discourages initiative, and weakens commitment to the work. At its worst it turns a human being into a semidetached circuit in a nonhuman production process and rewards the cultural ingot, whom the organization insulates from the realities of success and failure, usefulness and obsoleteness, efficiency and incompetence. In every case it represents the failure of an organization to motivate and utilize its most valuable asset—human resources.

The result? With the employee who tolerates the doomsday job, it spells professional ineffectuality. With the one who does not, it spells turnover.

An employee's dissatisfaction with the organization is rarely a reflection of maladjustment on his part or a sign of "natural" antagonism. Nor is quitting usually the result of rebellion or protest against any single act of management. "Bad" attitudes are more likely justifiable reactions to the work milieu and management's style and behavior. The factors that contribute to turnover and poor attitude must be changed in order to effect changes in the employee's viewpoint.

The personal reasons for turnover (relocation, health, change in marital status, and the like) account for a relatively small fraction of industry's turnover crisis. Pay is commonly used as a reason for termination, but as often as not it serves as a convenient way out. A company may find that workers in a given occupation category use pay as a reason for quitting more frequently than others. When this happens either there is a soft spot in the compensation program or a competitor has turned the organization into a training ground for his purposes. But when this reason is given by employees in many job classifications and particularly by high-potential management manpower, it signals real danger for the organization if those responsible do not look beyond the matter of pay.

What lies beyond the matter of pay is the key to turnover reduction: the understanding of human behavior and the application of this knowledge to the job situation. For management this must be the primary objective of the 1970s.

Motivation Theories

Among the earliest concerns of behavioral scientists was *why* people behave as they do. Attempts were made to list driving human forces, motivations, or needs. It became apparent that people seek to satisfy their needs. In the work sector of a person's life, this search focuses not only on the content of the job but on the environment—the professional relationships and physical surroundings associated with the work.

In the past the "gut responses" of the practitioner-manager comprised the only body of management knowledge. Today the art-*cum*-science of management is ever more willing to explore quantified research into human behavior, its causes, and the influences on it. Businesses are particularly attentive to studies of motivation and how it is affected by communication, leadership styles, and organization culture.

Motivation theories capture the imagination of business because of the relationship between the worker's motivation and improved productivity. Among the better-known, several of which will be discussed briefly in the following sections, are Douglas McGregor's Theory X and Theory Y; Maslow's needs hierarchy; Rensis Likert's linking pin and interaction influences theory, underscoring the crucial role of supervision in relation to group productivity; Argyris' mix model for integrating individual and organization objectives; R. R. Blake and J. S. Mouton's Grid®, charting the balance between the managerial variables of concern with people and concern with the task; and Herzberg's analysis of satisfiers and dissatisfiers. The theories have considerable potential for helping organizations reduce turnover and function more effectively in times of change.

McGregor's Theory X and Theory Y

Management has a knack of institutionalizing less productive methods when other alternatives are available, as the late Douglas McGregor illustrated with his Theory X–Theory Y concept.

The manager operating under Theory X views people as wanting to avoid work since work is not natural to them. He regards most human beings as individualists who are disinclined to cooperate with others. People are considered either unwilling or unable to make decisions. They can be trusted only so far, and if they are not treated like children, they will behave like hostile hordes. In sum people dislike work, must be forced into it, and would rather be told what to do than think for themselves.

Theory Y holds that people neither like nor dislike work but that their attitudes about it are based on their experiences with it. It also argues that people will pursue goals they believe in, play a part in setting, and are rewarded for reaching. It suggests further that under the proper circumstances people will seek responsibility since many possess and will exercise self-direction and high levels of creativity, imagination, and resourcefulness never tapped by industry.

The glaring difference between Theory X and Theory Y is the inflexibility of the former. Theory X management has few alternatives. It makes rules from which it allows no deviations; it creates feelings of dependence and guilt and threatens the economic and occupational security of the employee. At the time of the Industrial Revolution, its assumptions about how to manage people were thought to be valid: Given that the worker is fundamentally a child who dislikes work and is not wise enough to understand what is needed, threaten him and he produces; reward him by not threatening him.

It is not so much these erroneous assumptions that grate the sensitivities as it is the unwillingness of Theory X management to recognize that its rules do not fit *all* situations and *all* men. Its paternalistic rigidity implies that the failure of people to do its bidding is due to ethical or intellectual weakness. An attack on someone's ethics or intelligence invites the only possible response: to try to break or circumvent the control. Managers engage in this process daily without seeing the incredible phenomenon taking place because they are gamesmen in the confrontation. They view peak production capacity as the minimum acceptable quota; they consider it more important for an employee to clock in on time than to start working on time; they find it preferable for a worker to call in—falsely—that he is ill than to take a day off for personal reasons.

Doing away with rules and controls, time clocks and quotas will eliminate the *objects* of resentment and reaction. But will this encourage workers to produce more or get to work on time? Will it enable them to arrive at ethical and intellectual judgments about their work? Of course not. The problem is one of commitment and personal involvement—an internal kind of wanting.

The aim of Theory Y management is to stimulate internal motivation. Theory Y does not dictate a managerial style. It does not argue for soft approaches or giveaways; nor does it support rule breaking. It argues for an understanding of management's impact on people, urging a rational and relevant approach to employees that is flexible enough to accommodate the realities of their differing situations and their varying needs.

Maslow's Needs Hierarchy

One of the earliest and most important catalogs of human needs was Maslow's needs hierarchy, which is a synopsis of his theory of human motivation. Although challenged and modified, Maslow's theory remains a classic upon which many newer theories have been built. It was summarized by Douglas McGregor, and this summary has become the popular version of Maslow's thinking.

The basic premise of the needs hierarchy is that man is a wanting animal. No sooner is a need satisfied than another takes its place. Once satisfied, a need is no longer a motivator and ceases to be a driving force in a person's life, but it regains prominence if the satisfaction is threatened. A person does not concentrate on a higher-order need until those of the lower orders are satisfied.

The lowest order of needs is *physiological.* Man needs food, clothing, and shelter; he needs a job with which to earn money for these things for himself and his family.

When these needs are satisfied, he concerns himself with his *safety* needs. On the job he seeks protection against unfair management practices, arbitrary disciplinary action, discriminatory policies, and favoritism, for example. When he is highly dependent on the job, he seeks security satisfactions in the form of an even break.

Once these needs are satisfied, man turns his attention to the next higher order of needs, which are *social.* People want to belong; they want group identity and acceptance. Business has at times feared the formation of strongly knit work groups, incorrectly viewing these as hotbeds of potential hostility. Tightly knit teams can have a positive impact on work when the job environment is not hostile or overcontrolled.

Ego needs, the next higher order, represent man's view of himself and are never completely satisfied: the need for self-confidence and for recognition and respect from others. These needs are given little attention in the mass production organization. When left unsatisfied on the job, they are sought in off-the-job experiences.

The ultimate need, according to Maslow, is for *self-fulfillment* or *self-actualization*. This need represents man's striving to reach his full potential, his destiny as it were. But though it seems lofty and unattainable (and some insist that it is), it does not require achievements of epic proportions for satisfaction. On-the-job creativity, innovation, risk taking, and visible achievement are contributing satisfiers.

The daily struggle for economic survival and social and political equality deprives some people of the opportunity of ever moving beyond the lower levels of the hierarchy.

Herzberg's Satisfiers and Dissatisfiers

Herzberg's motivation theory proposes that motivation results from job satisfaction. The opposite of satisfaction is its absence rather than active displeasure. Thus satisfiers and dissatisfiers (or nonsatisfiers) can operate simultaneously and independently in a job.

Dissatisfiers are rules and policies, supervision, pay, working conditions, security, status, interpersonal relations, and other necessary and constant elements in every job environment. Dissatisfiers do not decrease or increase productivity but can reduce the worker's resistance, which in turn causes him to accept management's objectives passively.

These "pain avoiders," the hygiene factors on the job and in our lives, satisfy basic survival and safety needs. Note, however, that hygiene factors are external to the worker's specific job. Motivating factors—or satisfiers—arise from job content: opportunities for achievement, recognition, responsibility, and advancement. When only pain avoiders grow in an organization, the environment is being loaded, but job content is untouched.

Large, multilevel companies tend to become hygienic in their dealings with people. They impose rules and regulations that leave room for few exceptions, simplify jobs to facilitate measurement of performance, encourage rigid and bureaucratic management methods, and emphasize monetary and status rewards. Punishment may consist in anonymity or exclusion from the chain of communication. Innovation is considered disruptive and may lead to firing.

Some organizations publish detailed criteria for the successful performance of certain production, assembly, and clerical jobs. The theory is that employees are more secure when they understand precisely what is expected of them. This does help reduce misunderstandings, but it invites inflexibility on the part of supervisors who must appraise performance and creates a sterile work environment that disregards individual human differences. Hygienic conditions thwart initiative and risk taking, create defensiveness and secretiveness, and generally deprive the employee of opportunities to satisfy higher-order needs.

Enlightened supervisors and managers can turn many hygiene factors to advantage. Whereas rules usually indicate exactly *what* is expected of employees, they may not dictate *how* these predetermined objectives are to be achieved. While employees gain more commitment from participating to some degree in goal setting, autonomy in reaching the goals gives them some sense of involvement. The alert supervisor can evolve systems of job rotation and job enlargement in his department that will add a more human element to the rule-oriented, hygienic environment.

Motivation Methods

Despite the fact that managers have long been concerned about how to motivate workers, turnover figures indicate that their concern has borne inadequate fruit. One reason is resistance to change, as later chapters will discuss. Another is that organizations stubbornly hold to false ideas about what motivates people or apply proven concepts indiscriminately. A widespread and erroneous notion is that reducing the time spent at work is motivating. The fact is that a motivated employee wants more time on the job, not less. Potentially effective stimulators that have been used with dubious success range from money to rap sessions.

Economic Motivators

Money as a motivator is a mixed bag. Giving more and more money eventually fails to motivate and has led some managers to insist that if more wages will not work, perhaps less will. Money has therefore become both a threat and a lure, but at best it is an unpredictable means of motivating.

The economic man theory, that man works solely for financial gain, has fallen into disrepute. Yet it cannot be denied that the American culture puts a premium on money not only for what it buys but as a source of social recognition. Still, not all workers value money with the same intensity; nor are they likely to accept a job for more money without weighing the disadvantages.

Factory workers, as an example, often view bonuses, incentives, and premium rates for higher productivity and longer hours with suspicion. They recognize the utilitarian value of money for rent, clothes, food, and medical expenses (though they do not consider it the stairway to affluence). But they are fearful that more pay could lead to greater demands from management, cause layoffs because of inventory buildup, or invite automation as an economy measure and thus cost them their jobs. They are concerned that rate busting could create conflicts within the group and that longer work hours could affect health. In the final analysis the tradeoffs do not always seem worth the extra dollars.

Money may be the inducement to take a job; an increase may even delay an individual from quitting for a long period of time. But money cannot guarantee either job satisfaction or higher productivity. In addition sooner or later no more pay can reasonably be awarded if the company is to maintain an equitable compensation program, and an employee who has received an increase every six months, for example, will be disappointed, angry, and even hostile the first time he does not get a raise.

The same is true of cradle-to-grave benefits, which constitute 25 percent or more of the wage dollar. It would be nearly impossible to reverse the trend of security-oriented benefits. They are now seen as being "only human and decent." But like money, they feed insatiable desires for more. They must be constantly expanded or they create hostility. The fact is that benefit booms often backfire.

There is no residual benefit from salary increases. Increased income makes an employee happy, but there seems to be no more relationship between a happy worker and a productive one than between a company contribution for new bowling shirts and a more efficient worker. Motivation after all is an internal force or drive.

It is job content that is satisfying and that ultimately has the highest motivating influence. Money is not a part of job content. It is external to the job. Therefore, efficiency, productivity, and satisfaction are not always the long-term result of the lure of money.

Motivation from economic sources may be possible if the employee accepts the compensation program as enhancing or supporting his self-esteem and satisfying his ego needs. Perceptions of the equity of the system of compensation may have more motivating impact than the dollar amounts involved.

"Psychological" Techniques

It was reasonably easy for motivation-minded practitioners to build a bridge from humanitarian benefits to human relations. *Psychology* became the byword, and managers began "dealing" with employees. It became obvious that while employees indeed felt dealt with, productivity did not increase and motivation was not instilled. Employees became embittered because they felt management practices were phony; they doubted management's sincerity. Thus human relations approaches also failed to stimulate motivation.

But the failure gave rise to sensitivity and encounter training designed to help the motivator understand himself and *his* motives. When this too failed as a means of producing motivation in the employee, it was assumed that there was nothing wrong with sensitivity training but that the problem was one of communication, since employees failed to understand what management was trying to do. Communication techniques grew and communications specialists, house organs, bulletin boards, and briefings flourished. Still no motivation.

It was decided that the reason for this failure was one-way communication; there was no feedback from employees. Managers then turned to attitude surveys, suggestion plans, and gripe sessions. They got an earful, employees were happier, but nothing much improved in terms of motivation.

The next venture followed logically. It was felt that if employees could just get the big picture about their jobs, motivation was assured. It was not, of course. In order to gain a sense of achievement, a worker needs a job that makes that possible. If his entire job consists in tightening bolts, it does relatively little good to emphasize that he is a part of the automotive industry and a vital link in the manufacture of cars. He already knows that. Motivation through job participation failed because there was more concern given to "feelings" of participation and achievement than to tangible achievements associated with the job. Counseling only emphasized that management suspected there was something wrong with workers all along.

Limitations of Motivation Approaches

All these efforts to motivate reveal the same defect: the failure to transfer motivation from the manager to the worker. Workers can be badgered, threatened, loved, and lured without being motivated because all this activity originates with the manager, who is motivated, and is directed to the employee, who is not. Motivation must come from within the employee. In short he must want the same involvement as his manager or motivation has not taken place.

Many jobs do not lend themselves easily to motivation techniques. Production workers, controlled by the harsh realities of process engineering, need produce only the quota set by collective bargaining agreements, in-group consent, or managerial requirements, which are a function of the speed of the conveyor belt. The horizons of the production job are limited, and management, through its emphasis on technology and its union negotiating techniques, has indicated that it needs and desires no more.

Some employees do not want to achieve internal motivation. Their satisfactions are in the work environment or off the job. Their fulfillment may be in remaining third-generation factory workers who, through childhood and adult experiences, long ago adjusted to hygienic supervision in an organization. They may depend upon it.

Internal motivation is most readily developed in those whose work permits independence, who understand and accept their organization's objectives, and whose jobs are the central theme of their lives. This means professionals, managers, and only a few other categories of employees. Furthermore, despite its highly promising possibilities, motivation alone is not a panacea. If it is to be instilled successfully and durably, certain cultural norms and values in the organization must be changed, and this is both time-consuming and costly.

Nevertheless internal motivation is the best-known antidote to turnover because it prompts the individual to exercise a wide range of options through which to satisfy his needs. The limitations of this approach to job satisfaction do not negate its value to large numbers of high-potential people whose contributions are critical to the business operation. In fact these limitations should act as a challenge to manager-practitioners, researchers, and theorists to look beyond the present applications of internal motivation methods and seek effective means of bringing motivation to people on the production line.

The Impact of the Work Milieu

Job content, as motivation theorists of many stripes have emphasized, provides the employee with the foundation of his satisfaction in his work. The work may be varied, requiring judgment, imagination, and daring, or it may be repetitive, narrow, and predictable. Lower and middle managers often manifest strong needs for security, independence, and social or professional esteem; the job with variety would likely satisfy the employee driving for independence more than it would his security-seeking colleague.

But jobs do not exist in a vacuum. They operate in the physical and human surroundings of the organization as a whole. Studies have shown that low pay, a high proportion of female employees, and the absence of a union contribute to turnover, demonstrating that even relatively remote conditions influence the satisfaction people gain from their work. The closer the condition is to the performance of a job, the greater will be its bearing on the employee's needs.

The culture of the organization is the source of the most significant of these environmental factors or constants. The work may be performed in an informal, "small town" setting that requires no obvious sophistications and is characterized by strong group cohesiveness and group norms. The "urban" organization, on the other hand, may have an overstructured management hierarchy and utilize complex communications networks that put a premium on routine information and give the receiver a status not possible in the informal setting. The work culture may reinforce and reward variable needs such as aspiration level and desire for status to the exclusion of the more general lower-order needs.

These factors emanate from the organization at large and describe the work environment. Some are quantifiable and all are subject to analysis. Their importance lies obviously in the impact they have on the employee.

From the interface between the job proper and the work milieu arise what may be called interacting and intervening influences on the worker's behavior. They create feelings in the employee that move him to positive or negative action. Major categories are stress, which generates tension; thwarting, a cause of frustration; uncertainty, which activates anxiety; and contradiction, arousing a sense of conflict.

These influences are present in varying degrees on almost every job. In moderate doses they can enhance performance, but beyond a certain point—which differs from one person to the next—they become painful and can provoke quitting. Unless their dynamics are understood, their contribution to turnover will not be recognized, and efforts to solve the problem will be wasted.

Stress and Tension

Stress is an intervening influence occurring in the work environment that stimulates a response of tension from the worker. Stress can be caused by poor lighting or ventilation, noise, dangerous work conditions, long hours, and physical fatigue. But stress and the resulting tensions can arise from a series of failures or from job demands a worker believes are unreasonable. Its impact depends upon its duration, its causes, the attitude of the worker toward the leader and the causes, and what the worker believes is expected of him on his job.

Stress causes variable behavior, which may be unpredictable. People exhibit different thresholds of tension toleration. This threshold, which is a function partly of perception and partly of values and needs, determines how much stress a worker will take before it affects his behavior.

At first and at reasonable intervals, stress can improve performance and stimulate activity. When it continues, behavior changes sporadically and over a prolonged period can become aggressive, withdrawn, or disoriented. When the boss announces, for example, "We've got a big project to finish by Monday, and you'll have to work over the weekend," resistance is usually the first response. Following resistance and the temporary disorganization it produces, there is typically a period of return to normal behavior. If the weekend maximum efforts continue, coupled with additional stress and frustration (particularly if work done on a crisis basis must be redone or is not used), performance will decline, and there can be a total breakdown in the usual behavior patterns.

Stress is in large part controllable. The degeneration in behavior can be slowed or arrested and the breakdown averted if employees are involved in the problem and participate in its solution (here, work over the weekend). Studies have shown that the effects of stress can be reduced when workers have a healthy relationship with superiors, perceive support and active cooperation from them, and are provided with meaningful tangible or intangible rewards.

Thwarting and Frustration

An employee who quits because of frustration is responding to a somewhat different set of circumstances. Thwarting is a form of stress, but frustration differs from tension in that it is not generalized; it is a reaction to a specific obstacle to reaching a goal.

The most important negative effect of thwarting is that it can divert the worker from his challenge. "I've just been shot down" and "Back to the drawing board" are common expressions of frustration. Denial of a request for a change in assignment invites feelings of resentment and hostility because a goal has been thwarted. If the goal is an important one in the employee's hierarchy of needs, he may find it difficult to get over the experience. The result may be reduced quality and level of performance, a series of failures, and time off the job seeking other employment. The phrase *second effort*, associated with Vince Lombardi, the late coach of the Green Bay Packers and the Washington Redskins, shows how thwarting affects performance.

Frustration can be mitigated, of course, but this is difficult to do and depends heavily upon the supervisor-employee relationship. Assigning a person a difficult but highly visible and challenging project when promotion is denied may diminish deterioration in behavior while supporting the individual's adjustment.

Under certain circumstances thwarting can actively increase the amount of effort or drive people apply to the job. An employee's motivation to succeed can be so profound that nothing short of the challenge of a major obstacle will be satisfying. Thwarting can also clarify work requirements and help insure a high level and quality of performance. For example, in the early stages of employment or in the discovery phase of a project, it can define and reinforce efforts and skills required to reach the objective. It is particularly helpful when an employee displays overconfidence, works below his capacity, or demonstrates little interest in the "pushover" job.

Employees will remain goal-oriented despite repeated thwarting as long as there are alternate paths to the goal. They may even respond with renewed vigor after a series of frustrating blows. But if alternatives are unavailable and the duration of the goal thwarting is prolonged, frustration can heighten other negative feelings and produce disorganized behavior as a result of a damaged self-image and the denial of ego-need satisfactions.

Uncertainty and Anxiety

Anxiety is a response to uncertainty, which is also a form of stress but is future-oriented. Thus anxiety is concern or worry about what may or is likely to happen in the future. Anxiety is often linked to a cherished theme in a person's life. If the anxiety level can be kept within tolerable bounds, a high-anxiety worker usually performs better than a low-anxiety or failure-avoiding employee when the emphasis is on the importance of the work or task. But the low-anxiety person is the one who does best under fire and is rarely flustered.

In controlled doses uncertainty may be as stimulating as stress and thwarting. Studies have found that successful executives with strong achievement needs who are realistic, dynamic, adaptable to corporate life, and able to exhibit high objectivity experience feelings of anxiety in the form of apprehension that they will fail to meet company expectations.

But when uncertainty persists in an organization as a result of financial problems, poor communications, insecure leadership, or arbitrary and unfair management practices, the anxiety load becomes unbearable, and behavior breaks down. Employees can no longer differentiate between acceptable and unacceptable behavior or safe and harmful stimuli from the work environment. They become distracted easily from work, avoid decision making, problem-solve poorly, and are generally unadaptive. They play it safe, stifle imagination and initiative, and revert to habitual behavior—that is, to doing things they remember were once successful. Extreme anxiety can cause emotional disruption and psychosomatic illness.

Contradiction and Conflict

When employees are pulled in opposite directions emotionally, they are said to be in conflict. Conflict is a feeling provoked by contradictory environmental stimuli. It is the emotion that gives rise to expressions such as "Damned if you do and damned if you don't."

A seemingly simple way to resolve conflict is to rank incompatible drives or urges in order of importance or ease of gratification, satisfy one, and then face the next. But in organization life this may be difficult.

For example a boss orders, "Hurry up and change the filter on 108 and grease the chute." Both are important, take time, and must be done. But which comes first? The machine clogs if the filter is not changed, and this causes backup of the product. If the chute is not greased, the product will be damaged. Both result in product loss. Such a situation does not induce "good-good" conflict, as would choosing between buying a diamond or a ruby. It induces "good-bad" conflict in that either choice results in protection of the product at one point and loss of the product at the other. The behavior it prompts ranges from slowed execution of one task only—followed by post-decision conflict—to paralysis.

If the employee hesitates any length of time, the boss shouts, "Come on, don't you hear me? Get the lead out!" This prodding only heightens the conflict, and the struggle gains added proportions because the machine is clogging, backing the product up, and the product is sticking in the chute. The boss yells, "Hey, you, don't you follow orders? I won't tolerate insubordination." The employee's impulse is to strike out at him, which introduces new conflict. With a gasp of total despair, the employee runs from the work area, hopelessly withdrawing from the situation.

Productivity and Negative Environmental Influences

Productive behavior propelled by tension, frustration, and anxiety should not be confused with motivated behavior. The first is rigid and unadaptive and can deteriorate into random and unpredictable activity. The second is flexible and adaptive. Motivated people tend to exhibit rational control and freedom of choice, and their responses to challenges are means to ends. They are more sensitive to rewards, punishments, counseling, guidance, and training. These typically do not affect behavior under stress or the other environmental influences and may add to the negative feelings.

If the motivated response is relevant and purposeful, it is satisfying to the employee. But to the frustrated or tense individual, any response is a relief, even a destructive one. Obviously one of the most vital problems facing business organizations today is how to channel aggressiveness, the result of normal and abnormal strains on the job. Aggressive feelings can underlie a remarkable diversity of behavior patterns—lack of involvement or alienation and even termination among them.

It is naïve to expect that the negative elements in the work milieu will disappear and that employee and organization needs will somehow dramatically merge. They will not, despite tradeoffs on both sides and degrees of unhappiness for either or both. Only when unproductive behavior is recognized as a legitimate reaction to provocative stimuli emanating from the work environment can the organization's culture be humanized.

Behavior Telegraphs Needs

In practical terms how does an organization provide job satisfaction for employees? How in fact do people manifest their needs? Not everyone expresses the same need in the same way. Moreover there are many means of satisfying a given drive. Only through a person's behavior is it possible to gain reliable insight into what his needs are.

Yet even careful observation may be misleading. Witness these descriptions of behavior and the observers' interpretations—as opposed to the real causes.

Harry is the biggest apple polisher in the company. When he became Jensen's assistant, he grew a moustache just like Jensen's and started smoking pipes just like Jensen. He even taps his fingers like Jensen. Doesn't Harry have any self-respect? Of course he has self-respect, but he has an image problem that overpowers self-respect. He is identifying with Jensen, and this identification enhances his self-esteem.

Tom made his big pitch about that new program he had his heart set on, but it was rejected. Good old Tom—it didn't faze him in the least. He went back to his office, worked on the files, and even sat down at Millie's typewriter and banged out a letter. Frustrated in his attempts to reach an important goal and satisfy an achievement need, Tom reverts to performing clerical rather than managerial duties.

Bob is a bad sort. He just doesn't care about his job. Bob has received no praise, recognition, or reward for his hard work, and so he has broken off emotional contact with the job. His apathy is a withholding of personal involvement.

Phil keeps checking the financial statement for accuracy even though it's a computer printout. He's stubborn or stupid. Some people never get the message. Phil got the message that his opinions were not valued when no one consulted him before the company bought the new computer. Phil is exhibiting a nonadjustive reaction to an irreversible situation.

Interpreting employees' behavior is complicated further by the fact that a specific satisfaction may correspond with different needs in different people. Promotion is a case in point. Two people who are promoted may react similarly. They are happy and momentarily satisfied. But the first may need the money that the advance brings while the second may need authority and status. Suppose the first employee gets a promotion that gives him prestige and no money while the second receives money and no prestige. Both will be dissatisfied, and if in time they perceive no hope of fulfilling their wants, their behavior will reflect their unhappiness.

Cultural differences will of course affect the priority of needs. Suppose a third employee who is the son of an immigrant family also receives a promotion. During his formative years the central themes of his life were survival and the protection of hard-won gains. Neither money nor power may have central import to him. Instead the *fact* of the promotion may give him satisfaction by reinforcing physiological and safety needs.

Each person develops a personal style for meeting his needs. Gratifying actions, those that bring satisfaction, are repeated; approaches that create displeasure are not repeated. In addition the individual sets up defense mechanisms (which are part of his personal style) to guard against punishments in the form of satisfaction denial. By these means he attempts to exert some degree of control over the job itself and the work environment. The behavior patterns that make up his style of dealing with his needs tell the observant organization how best to build satisfactions into his work.

Job Satisfaction and Turnover

Despite efforts in recent years to take the doom out of jobs, many obstacles to job satisfaction remain in the modern business organization. Workers are still given orders without reason or justification that are based on decisions they play no part in reaching. Opportunities to participate in problem solving and planning are denied to most workers, who thus continue to have little if any control over factors affecting their occupational and ultimately their private lives.

The impact of this deprivation is greatest on those with the largest potential contribution to make to the organization—college graduates, skilled technicians, and achievement-oriented people over 30. These are the workers who will feel the deepest sense of discontent and disappointment when placed in doomsday jobs, and these are the workers most likely to respond to their lack of satisfaction by quitting. But doomsday elements beset most other classifications of employees as well.

Mass production has caused job content and other major satisfiers to be engineered out of factory jobs. The price management pays for simplifying operations is lack of worker pride, low worker aspiration levels, and a hygienic work environment. Factory work also provides few opportunities for important social relationships on the job that reduce boredom and allow the worker to function as a total personality. His alienation from his company makes him susceptible to job openings in other firms that offer marginally improved conditions.

Why Executives Quit

That executive turnover is high is a fact of corporate life. Managers increasingly identify more with their occupations than with their employers, which is a major reason that they have become one of the most mobile occupation groups in the nation. When frustrated they move on because they are able to find work elsewhere, and they prefer to shift jobs rather than attempt to improve their current situation.

Not always are their moves successful, and it is fairly common to observe a series of short-term employments revealing a pattern of hurried selection on the part of both the company and the manager. The fact that these mistakes can be made and the individual remain marketable is an indicator of the executive turnover problem.

Often a manager's quitting can be linked to his evaluation of his prospects for professional growth and profit with a company. An aggressive, competent young employee who sees managers at the top not much older than he is may fear blockage and flee, sometimes despite enrichment and development opportunities, preferring more upward mobility potential even in a more confining job.

Job content has primary importance for the executive. It takes the simple pleasure out of his work if he is assigned responsibility without authority, involved in so many meetings that he cannot do his proper work, subjected to arbitrary and unfair judgments by top management, and loaded with more tasks than he can reasonably accomplish with care and pride.

The executive needs corporate love and attention. When nepotism, cronyism, or paternalism makes him feel unwanted or unappreciated, he looks for "better" employment situations. Close, smooth communication and feedback with the boss are important for the young executive. He wants more than vague rapport and occasional telephone calls, initialed notes, and conference-style conversations. He wants an appraisal of where he stands in terms that are meaningful to him personally, not a translation of a performance rating system in which his entire being is reduced to a point spread of 1 to 5. If he is treated like a nonentity, he will seek a job where his efforts will give him a higher profile.

Politics is of course a major reason for executives' quitting, particularly when it affects promotions, assignments, work locations, and salary. Politics can also drive a man out by denying him recognition or encouraging slights in disregard of his personal sensitivities.

An organization can vitalize its managers' sense of affiliation in a number of ways. Executives usually respond well to proprietorship arrangements, whether these consist of participating in the decision-making process or making a phantom stock venture successful. Well-paced training and development programs that strike a practical balance between skills required now and those needed in the future make the executive feel a sense of permanence. Well-timed salary increases are important, but compensation systems that tie together personal income needs, corporate profits, and the executive's contribution come closest to giving him a feeling of ownership.

Enriching the Doomsday Job

Doomsday jobs of every complexion have a common characteristic: they limit rather than activate the employee's potential. Every human being has a capacity for growth. The stimuli of growth are motivation, past achievement, and future opportunities. The challenge to the organization is to extend the horizons of the job so that it provides increasing responsibility, appropriate recognition of accomplishment, and the possibility of advancement. These are the components of successful job enrichment.

Enriching the job, however, is not the same as enlarging it. Job enlargement simply amplifies what exists on the job but does not enhance its development aspects. Examples of enlargement are an increase in production demands, the addition of duties that differ from the basic job only in detail rather than substance, and job rotation that merely shifts duties.

A doomsday job stultifies. Its antithesis, the enriched job, offers variety, independence, and the chance to use skills in an unstructured, autonomous way. It is the job built to human dimensions.

TWO

renewing the doomsday organization

DOOMSDAY organizations are those in which doomsday jobs are allowed to flourish. These are companies willing to tolerate human waste and the loss of productivity and profits caused by high turnover rather than rid the organization culture of the values and practices that make such jobs possible.

It is sometimes difficult to assess the state of a company's cultural health. The marginal doomsday organization is one in which few doomsday jobs exist. This is of relatively minor concern except to the employee who happens to hold a job devoid of content or embedded in an alienating work milieu.

Full-blown doomsday organizations, regardless of their advanced technologies, remain at the Industrial Revolution stage in their regard for and maintenance of people. They have not gone through an improvement process perhaps because of too little profit, abundant profit over a long time, or unenlightened leadership. They exhibit courage and determination in their efforts to overcome the obstacles of turnover costs on the bumpy road to profit, but they will not take decisive steps to change the administrative processes, policies, and organization structure that are the causes of job dissatisfaction. Indeed such organizations can often be found to increase the number of people who either perform unproductive work or quit by rewarding those who collaborate with the failing system and punishing those who don't.

It has been argued that organization changes should be prompted more by external threat and internal deterioration than by an active search for problems, that renewal should not be undertaken until stresses and constraints on habitual organizational behavior are felt. The argument is that these provide realistic indications of need and prevent change for the sake of change—unnecessary and even harmful tampering with successful methods. Signs of deterioration should therefore serve as meaningful indicators of the organization's performance.

The danger in this approach is that it presupposes exceptional sensitivity to employees' needs—a quality for which few organizations are noted. In effect a company with such a viewpoint may not be aware of doomsday elements in its jobs until it has begun to lose workers. Turnover puts the organization into a state of flux as new behavior patterns and interpersonal expectations are introduced. While this can create healthy challenge and rejuvenation, it also produces disruption in the organization. The resulting stress and uncertainty can cause even greater job dissatisfaction for employees and managerial inflexibility in human relations practices, and these in turn tend to increase turnover.

Organizations that commit themselves to renewal discover new ways to solving problems and generate new behavior patterns. The improvement process encourages employees to analyze organization inadequacies in a free and open communication system as an ongoing part of corporate life. Thus renewal is a self-perpetuating function.

Renewal does not occur simply because management wants it to. It is a patient and orderly process of study, planning, and action that changes the values and practices behind profit-draining human waste and eliminates doomsday jobs.

Centralized versus Decentralized Organizations

Any discussion of organization action to eliminate doomsday jobs must be concerned with the structures that support the human relationships among its members. Organization structures are after all a system of human relations based upon a source of authority at the top. Organizations spread horizontally because of the division of labor, which results in varying degrees of specialization.

There is vertical stress in the organization from the exercise of authority; there is also horizontal stress from the interplay of organization and worker objectives. The organization evolves on the basis of its overall business needs and those of its people. When human needs are emphasized, business objectives may suffer. When company needs are emphasized, it can take a human toll.

Management—meaning the development and the utilization of the workforce—entails a constant balancing of these vertical and horizontal stresses, which can never be eliminated, if the organization as an entity is to survive. In terms of both productivity and job satisfaction, decentralization has proved more successful than centralization in promoting a healthy equilibrium in the organization structure.

Functional Relationships

Every organization, whether centralized or decentralized, has both formal and informal elements. The organization as a whole is a composite of these substructures. However, one or the other will predominate.

The decentralized organization recognizes and capitalizes on the influence of informal substructures. Consultative and mutually supportive informal groups arise from the motivation of individual workers to solve problems in their own way. These informal groups often have access to all management levels. Not to be found on the organization chart and rarely named, they provide important communication channels both vertically and horizontally.

In decentralized organizations the informal work groups as well as the departments or other formal subdivisions are allowed to be as inclusive as possible. This self-sufficiency encourages delegation and job enrichment. It also brings about employee understanding of corporate objectives and interdepartment problems and of the relationships between their jobs and the department as well as between the department and the external organization.

Interaction among employees and fluidity of communication characterize the way the work gets done in the decentralized organization. Employees are given latitude to identify and solve problems confronting them. This breeds a sense of identity and personal commitment that can never exist in the centralized organization, in which people fail to get the big picture. The implications for motivation and for reduced turnover are obvious.

Functional relationships are constrained in the predominantly centralized structure. Formal reporting channels and controls hedge job performance and enforce a strict division of labor. Leadership and responsibility are not shared, and rules, policies, and work specifications operate at the expense of group norms and individual needs.

Management and Supervision

Centralized organizations adopt a mechanistic approach to management. This takes one or both of two forms. The first is the establishment of an organization plan that describes reporting relationships and lists all job responsibilities and objectives. The second and often accompanying form is the aggregation of common job functions or clearly related skills under one supervisor or manager.

The mechanistic approach does not guarantee either productivity or the development and involvement of people. Sometimes the result is quite the contrary. Intergroup conflict often arises because all jobs within a department are highly specialized. Supervisors tend to be more results- than process-oriented and rarely feel called upon to analyze the causes of either success or failure.

The mechanistic approach tends to be hygienic and paternalistic. Authoritarian management styles gain momentum through successive layers of the organization. Supervisors keep delegation to a minimum because of the narrow specialties in the departments for which they are responsible and because of rigid job specifications. Moreover, performance appraisals place little value on their ability to delegate. As a result workers and management personnel are relatively inflexible and nonadaptive. Cooperation is rarely spontaneous either within or between departments. There is usually a high superior-subordinate ratio because supervision is procedure-oriented and the span of control is based upon predetermined assumptions rather than determined by individual differences among managers and variations in the work load. Middle and lower management and their subordinates have little opportunity for horizontal interaction; supervision is largely a mediating effort in which a balance is struck between hygienically structured communications from above and workers' needs for motivating, satisfying, and supportive communication.

Organizations such as these tend to resist change and cling to the status quo. Initiative is discouraged because change requires multiple levels of approval. It is not uncommon to see numerous signatures, even including the chief executive officer's, on a payroll advice authorizing a routine salary increase. Doomsday jobs proliferate in such a work environment.

Organizations less centralized need fewer managers and supervisors because managerial responsibilities are broadened and decision making, problem solving, and goal setting take place at the lowest possible levels. Unlike centralized organizations, which operate from power bases through a hierarchical chain of command, modern decentralized organizations are controlled from the bottom up rather than from the top down; they are built upon functional interrelationships among individuals and departments.

Supervision is conceptualized in terms of who does the work and how it is to be coordinated at the lowest possible level rather than what work is to be done and how to channel it in a specified procedural mode. The role of the department manager is thus enlarged in scope and importance. He is much more than the chief technician or practitioner. A major aspect of his work is to analyze job functions in relation to the behavior necessary to achieve success. This sensitivity achieves human compatibility with job requirements.

Job Descriptions and Procedures

In the centralized organization structure, job descriptions and procedures by which jobs are performed tend to be inviolable. They are rarely changed or modified. As a matter of pride and out of inflexibility, centralized organizations refuse to adapt jobs to people. It is not uncommon to hear managers speak indignantly about applicants who try to bend the organization to *their* will.

Centralized organizations may attempt to bring the employee into more personal encounter with the hierarchical system by providing channels such as attitude surveys, bulletin boards, house organs, and various management-worker committees and counsel groups. While these efforts can alleviate stress in the work milieu, they are tradeoffs for true participation and involvement.

Jobs are rarely enriched in this setting. Job training, which predominates almost to the exclusion of worker training, is aimed at increasing job skills and procedural know-how, with only minimal attention given to process, theory, and general management and administrative techniques. This emphasis is based on the false assumption that a worker who is proficient at his job is happier and more productive. But happiness cannot be equated with productivity and is not a reliable source of motivation, as discussed in Chapter 1.

Decentralized organizations seek people whose personalities are compatible with job demands, in addition to requiring necessary prerequisite skills and experience. To provide a realistic example, typical interview questions that reflect this point of view would be "Can you add columns of figures rapidly and with accuracy? And do you like to?" Jobs are also analyzed in terms of the need for human interaction with other people or groups, the frequency of these contacts, and the intensity.

Some decentralized companies will go farther and change the emphasis within a job, shift responsibilities, and even rearrange the functions of several jobs. This enriches and enlarges the work for those involved, reinforces the organic human system, and provides for human differences.

People Orientation: Arguments, Counterarguments

Organization theorists who favor the people orientation fostered by decentralization argue that the corporate structure has a dramatic effect on human relations and that decentralization enables a company to accommodate the day-to-day demands on employees realistically. They point out that though the emphasis on the worker aspect of business changes the focus of the manager, traditional executive qualities of decisiveness, profit-mindedness, and ambition are still valued. The added dimension is the ability to generate close working relationships among individuals, to facilitate cooperation between groups with different objectives, and generally to maintain sensitivity to the human side of business.

This emphasis on the man in management is challenged by those who believe that it complicates relatively simple supervisor-subordinate relations, intrudes upon employees' personal values, is manipulative, and puts workers' welfare ahead of shareholders' interests. They argue that all considerations are secondary to the primary purpose of the business organization, which is to make profit for its owners. In their view the people orientation of the decentralized organization creates disruption and instability and constitutes an accommodation that business should not be expected to provide. One cannot wholly disregard these arguments, but they do not prevail.

People orientation does not make a manager a coward, an altruist, or a fool. If this were true, employees would never be fired or disciplined, and companies would never fight competitively in the market.

Manipulation is possible when an insincere manager or supervisor misuses group action techniques to hide his paternalistic or authoritarian tendencies. But employees are not stupid and are sensitive to phonies, and they have alternative courses of action and freedom of choice. In addition they have information sources beyond the confines of the organization. The pronouncements of management can always be verified and challenged either at the department level or through unions. Moreover management and labor want mutually acceptable methods to respond to problems because they have a vested interest in the survival of the organization. For this reason a motivated workforce serves a company's stockholders well: its goal is to make the business operate successfully, which means profitably. In the long run the preservation of jobs is a strong mediating factor.

Resistance to Organization Change

Although the pressure to change mounts over the years, organizations resist because of forces within their culture that stifle response to the need for change.

Studies have shown that the less successful managers in an organization are readier to seek change than the more successful. This is because executives high in the organization hierarchy hesitate to modify the system that has treated them well. They may experience role conflict when called upon to promote organization renewal for the common good because it puts them in confrontation with norms and practices that have brought them success and that they may have helped establish. Unsuccessful managers sometimes seek change because they feel they have nothing to lose. But the valuable manager is the one committed to solving the turnover problem, a responsibility that rests more heavily on him the higher he stands on the organization ladder. It is he who must activate and sustain the renewal process after objectively evaluating all the facts and insuring the orderly and intelligent implementation of change.

Organization renewal can also be delayed and even thwarted by middle and lower managers and workers, who must ultimately be responsible for the key data gathering and group problem solving required for change. These employees are in a position to distort information and procrastinate. Change after all could weaken and even destroy delicate relationships carefully cultivated through the years with superiors, subordinates, and peers. Pet methods that they have developed and that have gained them recognition could be discredited or even abolished.

Employees who do see the need for renewal may not equate *organization* change with *department* change. Even though organization change is the foundation of improvement, they personally identify with department change as their immediate source of satisfaction.

First-line supervisors may fear that their leadership will be threatened or weakened by the open communications networks that organization renewal builds. They may feel cut off from the people for whom they are responsible and from the central management process when open channels of communication allow them to be circumvented. They may also be concerned that organization renewal will introduce an even greater degree of specialization (which they sense as narrowing) into their work by reducing them to chief technicians rather than managers of people.

As the renewal process is inaugurated, employees at all levels find themselves groping for new behavior norms. The dynamics of change dictate that in the early stages there are varying degrees of disorientation, breakdown in the existing value system, and other negative effects. The benefits of change—increased job satisfaction for the employees and a marked decline in turnover—are future outcomes that follow trauma, a period of increased costs and internal stress.

During this period even upper-level managers tend to be reluctant to undertake the renewal process wholeheartedly because they fear that the old reward and punishment system may be invoked at any time. They seek signs that such will not be the case and that top management indeed means what it says about renewal. Only through time will top management prove the seriousness of its purpose, not by what it says but by actions.

The Manager as Change Agent

Organizational change that eliminates doomsday jobs occurs when the behavior of the organization's leaders on all strata is modified. Managers throughout the company should understand the impact of their roles as change agents. This insight is the foundation of their commitment to renew the organization.

Commitment requires a deeper emotional reaction than agreement. Agreement represents simply a lack of negativity toward an issue;

people go along, meeting requirements they are told to meet, exhibiting "sufficient" positive behavior but little more. Commitment results when feelings of ownership are aroused in managers. It is reinforced as they participate in problem solving and decision making pursuant to the initial decision to effect important change.

The mandate for renewal must of necessity come from the top, but renewal is a process. This means that managers on all echelons must not only lead subordinates toward new behavior patterns but provide feedback to superiors on the effectiveness of the changes that are occurring.

The renewal process is thus tantamount to a learning circuit on which each manager functions as both educator and student. For this reason his role as change agent consists of more than acting as resource to a task force or working with a management group or problem-solving team. He must himself develop and inspire in others a new sense of identity, one that lessens local loyalties and encourages the evolution of more effective behavior patterns.

Behavior changes as a result of learning experiences that give people alternative ways of acting. The focus of the educator's concern is not on whether people will learn; they will. The important point for organization renewal is what they learn and how, for the education process exerts as much influence on behavior as what is taught.

Learning, much like organization renewal, requires that the learner discover a deficit that he needs to fill or a flaw that he wishes to correct. His perception of his future possibilities establishes a goal. He then takes postive steps to reach this goal by seeking learning opportunities. He responds to the learning experiences on the basis of his ability, his achievement during and after the learning process, and others' appraisals of his learning performance. When the learner attains his goal, he can behave in ways he previously could not.

A Key Problem: Changing Attitudes

High priority in the learning process must be given to uncovering and correcting erroneous management attitudes about workers. Attitudes are favorable or unfavorable prejudgments. They assume an idea, condition, or object to have an unchanging nature, good or bad, and they find expression in verbal and nonverbal behavior. When attitudes are formed around a central theme, they constitute a person's value system.

Managers' attitudes concerning job functions, worker motivation, and their own inviolable rights as managers are often defense mechanisms that protect them from acknowledging that their methods of operation have not proved successful. They may adhere to traditional management styles in an effort to give rational meaning to their job needs and to maintain their footing in their ambiguous role as someone's employee and someone's boss. Regardless of why managers cling to marginally successful or even unsuccessful methods, the challenge is to modify the attitudes that underlie their behavior.

Merely indicating that change is needed is futile. Telling a manager that he has an ineffectual behavior pattern, describing the attitudes it demonstrates, and expecting an overnight reform will accomplish nothing. The manager needs learning experiences that show him *how* to modify his behavior. These have a ricochet effect: As he engages in activities aimed at heightening his effectiveness, he will displace old attitudes with new ones shaped by the more successful behavior.

The formation of the new attitudes arises out of new perceptions that the manager gains from his learning experiences. Perceptions are the way people see the world. Whether a person's perceptions are accurate or not is usually of little importance to him as long as they help him understand and control his environment. Most people show common understandings about perceptual stimuli. This is what makes effective communications and predictions about behavior possible.

Behavior and understanding about the environment change only as a function of a broadening of the perceptual field. What people do not perceive they cannot act upon. What they do perceive adds to the storehouse of information they possess about the world surrounding them and modifies their attitudes.

Attitude change takes time and persistent encouragement. The learning process must be free of negative elements. One of the quickest ways of thwarting change and causing reversion to habitual patterns of thinking is to warn, "You'll come around," or to comment when change is noted, "I knew you'd come to your senses." Any person involved in attitude change must be allowed to maintain his self-respect and his standing in the group. Loss of credibility should not be the cost of changed attitudes.

The formation of new attitudes can be accelerated by praise of the new behavior from superiors and peers. This adds to the feelings of satisfaction the manager derives from the improved efficiency and productivity of his workforce that result from his new ability to instill motivation.

Peer pressure can have considerable impact. When one manager is continuing to think in terms of job specifications, quotas, and authority while his associates are talking about job satisfactions, human needs, and communication, their example will strongly influence his frame of reference. So will making the dissenter chairman of the committee, an old but effective way of helping modify attitudes.

Team Efforts

The doomsday organization begins the renewal process by becoming aware of problems and dedicating itself to solving them. Perhaps the most effective method of carrying out the renewal is to assign task forces or study groups composed of both administrative and operations managers the responsibility of analyzing problems, needs, and opportunities in all parts of the organization.

The effectiveness of the team approach is due to the fact that organizations are composed of functionally related groups, after all, not individuals working in isolation. Change is therefore facilitated by group problem solving and other group action. The teamwork overcomes natural barriers to open expression and interchange of ideas and strengthens communications networks. Individuals experience more growth in the open group, which is supportive and encourages trust. Their defensiveness is lessened, with a proportionate decrease in alienation, secretiveness, and conflict.

The renewal process is sometimes aided by a consultant retained by the organization, who provides objectivity in monitoring activities, guidance, and counsel but does not become an active participant in the improvement process as such.

Task Forces

The task forces inaugurating the renewal process are given the mission of evaluating and making recommendations about training and development, turnover, the financial reporting system, benefits, market sensitivity and feedback services, technological advances and obsolescence, and so forth. Each task force contains a mix of management members from all disciplines within the organization. This promotes communication among otherwise dichotomous groups and helps break down traditional barriers to understanding. Each task force must receive the mandate of the chief executive officer of the organization and a ranking corporate officer in the division in which it is deployed.

The chairman of the task force may be a manager whose functional responsibility is in an area in which renewal is sought. For example, the director of manpower planning might chair the turnover task force, the controller, the financial reporting system group, and the employment manager, the promotion and advancement team. Department heads who chair task forces and in whose functional areas improvement opportunities are sought lose no authority or responsibility; quite the contrary.

Leadership within the task forces is not a matter of personality or title but rather the functional role of group members. Problems are solved using methods the groups find appropriate to their style and the subjects at hand.

Several or all of the task forces may find it helpful to form subcommittees composed of employees in departments and functions affected and chaired by the department head or supervisor. These subgroups issue written reports or recommendations to the parent task force. In this manner all or most members of the organization become involved in the work of renewal.

The result of identifying problems and summarizing the needs and opportunities facing the company is a set of realistic recommendations whose formulation is recognized as an achievement for all the people in the organization. These recommendations represent the best thinking of the organization about its future.

The task forces may be disbanded after their recommendations have led to objectives. However, the spirit of commitment of many task forces demands their continuation as an important part of the informal organization and an excellent two-way communications medium for management. They then become an ongoing resource in department and corporate planning, implementation, and followup. The result is a toning up of department performance and a continuing and vital sense of purpose.

Participation and Involvement

The team approach allows a large number of organization members to participate in the renewal process. Their task force work provides them with recognition and opportunities for need satisfaction. It insures their involvement and support and opens communications channels throughout the organization. These efforts also help identify managers who exhibit outstanding performance under this new form of corporate problem solving.

Each group member is a resource to every other member. Data used to isolate problems, set priorities, and help focus on areas deserving future attention are fed from one group to another so that the responsibilities for problem solving are shared. This stimulates planning and objective setting, functions that are often denied to organization members below the top-management level.

What results is a development process by which the organization augments its problem-solving capabilities at the same time that it utilizes its employees' full resources, thus enriching their jobs and tapping their sense of commitment. As the process continues, the organization becomes a well-integrated, self-correcting system of interfunctional relationships. The doomsday job will not exist in such an environment.

The Purpose of Renewal

By examining its present methods and values, the organization intervenes in its operations to discover more effective alternatives. The overall purpose is not to improve systems but to maximize human potential. The human-oriented approach argues that businessmen must consider human welfare as a dimension of equal rather than subordinate concern to the realm of machines and technology. This attitude awakens a sense of proprietorship in employees that reinforces their commitment to the organization's goals as well as their trust in its leadership.

It may never be possible to integrate the goals of the company and those of the individual completely. But it is possible to create a work environment designed to satisfy the growth needs of employees. It has been shown that when avenues are opened that make it possible for people to realize their potential in their work, their satisfaction will not only keep them in the job but induce them to give it their best efforts.

Contrary to the objections of some critics, therefore, emphasis on the human dimension thus does not undermine the classic reason for a business' existence: to make profits for shareholders through productivity. The human dimension is an enabling factor for business; doomsday organizations are disabling.

THREE
technical specialization

THIS IS the age of specialization, a phenomenon so common that it is often taken for granted as a natural way of life. Specialization narrows a work function to repetitive though sometimes complex activity that continues virtually unchanged throughout a person's entire career. It magnifies the doomsday elements in an organization and creates new dissatisfactions of its own.

In vast, technologically oriented industries such as the automotive, aerospace, electronics, and chemical, specialists flourish. Employees with advanced degrees in specialties apply themselves to narrow if professionally challenging jobs dealing with a minute segment of a huge research program or one of hundreds of components of a product.

Specialists often lack mobility, however. Production workers, assemblers, and clerks who perform a single task over and over are also considered specialists. While they can generally adapt their basic skills to other jobs, it is often impossible for them to transfer to another job even in the same department without retraining.

Specialization on assembly lines and in many clerical jobs results in short-cycle tasks that can be performed in seconds or minutes. This cyclical repetition eliminates all sense of stimulation from the work. But nonproduction workers experience the same deprivation. There is little opportunity to dwell on an interesting problem or experiment with innovative approaches because of deadlines and because the backlog of work that might result would tie up dependent functions. Thus many employees, even in responsible management positions, find it difficult or impossible to vary their methods or the pace of work.

It would be a mistake to view specialization problems as afflicting solely centralized organization structures. Decentralized businesses struggle with them as well. Specialization has brought with it difficulties in lateral relationships, the chain of command, communications, and role definition (particularly for the line manager). However, the human orientation and flexibility of decentralized organizations make them better able than centralized firms to deal effectively with problems in all employee classifications affected by specialization—task specialists and professionals themselves, the groups that make up specialized departments, and generalist managers.

Task Specialization

Task specialization in industry is the usual result of job simplification. Jobs are reduced to their basic elements. These elements are distributed among various workers as widely as needed to make each task quick to learn.

One advantage of this is less duplication of expensive equipment and thus lower capital expenditures. The company acquires smaller and cheaper but more specialized pieces of equipment that allow each element of the job to be done repetitively on a small scale.

Task specialization is usually seen as a way to predict productive behavior with high accuracy. Job controls are more precise because production records, quality checks, process engineering, and performance appraisal can be applied to a narrow job segment with few confusing variables and intangibles intervening.

Obviously training costs are reduced because less time is required to teach a limited task than a complex job. While turnover rates may be high, most replacements can be trained within a few days or weeks and brought to the breakeven point quickly. It is also possible to hire less skilled people, who command lower wages. High degrees of specialization tend to curtail wasted time because the worker usually remains at a work station and need not move about or adapt to other tasks.

Task specialization in sum is a technology-based method of job simplification that calls on a limited range of skills and purports to increase efficiency and productivity. However, it creates doomsday jobs in abundance by reducing morale, motivation, and satisfaction and denying workers recognition, development, and advancement opportunities. The most immediate effect of any specialized task is boredom.

Boredom and Its Byproducts

Many production jobs, nearly all assembly work, and a large portion of clerical duties consist of relatively low-attention tasks. They are so routine that the worker's mind wanders to other things while he performs his job.

Workers move through various stages of attention. In the learning stage there is considerable concentration until the job is learned. With proficiency attention levels lessen, and ultimately fantasies or other mental wanderings capture the worker's mind as a defense against the boredom. But at least daydreaming on the job can help break the monotony. Tasks that require some degree of alertness are worse because the worker cannot escape the repetition by turning his thinking elsewhere.

The specialized task is unlike professional work and other jobs that stimulate involvement and provide challenge over long periods of time. These often increase the employee's depth of attention because of the numerous unexpected occurrences and continued self-development that result from the work itself.

Mass production and many clerical jobs often seem endless to the worker because these jobs lack a sense of accomplishment. Workers do not feel they are exercising a skill. The jobs can be learned readily and performed by most people.

The task specialist is not to be confused with the skilled craftsman, who today is a rare specimen. The specialist has little freedom to choose the style, speed, or technique of his work—important factors, as studies show clearly that when workers can vary their pace and develop a natural rhythm, they are more satisfied and less bored and fatigued. People performing specialized tasks exercise little judgment about their work because engineering specifications narrow the scope of the job. Assembly workers for example may develop tricks of the trade, but these are limited. Skilled craftsmen on the other hand require minimal supervision, gain recognition from their work, and exercise initiative and imagination. Task specialists are more highly controlled and find few opportunities for self-expression through the work itself. Their jobs offer few possibilities for variety or innovation.

The mass production worker is often embarrassed by the simplicity of his job and tends to exaggerate its difficulty. He rarely sees or understands the entire production process or work system. Job satisfaction is slight and the sense of accomplishment limited. Yet some do cleave to such jobs. Who are they?

Who Sticks with the Specialized Task?

Workers of course differ in what they expect from a job. Studies have shown that people with high intelligence and with extroverted personalities typically quit monotonous jobs. Other employees are quite happy with routine work. They want no challenge, feel secure in doing a specific task in a specific way at a specific time, and would be disturbed and would possibly flee the situation if required to do more. This type of worker often scoffs at the thought that mass production is fundamentally destructive of morale and limits human capacity.

People who derive some degree of satisfaction from monotonous jobs usually do so through social relationships in the work environment, not through the work itself. There are those who make a game of the work by seeing it as something to do with their hands. Many women consider their jobs not as work but rather as hobbies. Women planning to marry are often content with routine jobs because they lack career objectives and see the job as a means to a short-range objective, usually financial. Working mothers want to fill their time between breakfast and dinner when the family comes together again. Older workers counting the days until retirement and young men awaiting induction into military service are likely to tolerate high degrees of specialization on a routine job. Others who find such jobs acceptable are people who lack adjustment to family and the home.

Professional Specialization

Professional specialization involves career-oriented fields of technical or technological knowledge. These provide considerable opportunities for job identification, motivation, and development. These jobs are not fragmented. Many require multiple levels of skills and know-how. Yet even these jobs may breed considerable discontent and problems within the human organization.

Experts and Advisers

Organizations of any size hire specialists whose responsibility it is to give information and advice to line and staff operations and in some cases to function as group directors. All employees develop area expertise on the job; the specialist differs in that he has had formal preparation, usually through advanced education, in his field. Small firms with a limited number of employees and large companies with a periodic need or an important problem to solve may retain outside consultants.

Line and staff experts differ considerably in terms of the satisfactions each receives from his work. The staff adviser typically takes no action and makes no decisions. He supplies technical information to decision makers. His achievement satisfactions are foreshortened. The line adviser on the other hand not only supplies technical advice but may be placed in charge of a special project. While it is possible to find exceptions to these distinctions, it is important to note that in each case the sense of achievement each specialist gets is at a different point on the problem-solving continuum.

There may be in fact only a narrow line between supplying advice and giving facts. A member of the personnel department may be responsible for developing turnover data. How he carries out his task depends upon whether his organization is decentralized and human-oriented or centralized and procedure-oriented. He may supply data in neatly typed columns and have satisfied his job requirements. On the other hand he may produce these figures, analyze them verbally, and even make written recommendations for correcting the problem.

The two procedures meet the specialist's needs at different points on the problem-solving continuum. The person who satisfies his needs by producing columns of perfectly calculated numbers may not enjoy the challenge of analyzing the numbers or taking risks by offering opinions about what they mean. Conversely the person interested in analytical problem solving and risk taking will become unhappy if his job requires only research but blocks any further involvement.

The Authority Roles of Specialists

The classic picture of authority emanating from the top of an organization and working its way down to subordinates who obey gives way in the case of the specialist. As specialization increases, lateral relationships between specialty departments become more significant. More than simple horizontal peer relationships, specialty groups that are functioning well develop strong coordinating links with one another to prevent the slowing of production, redundant record keeping, needless competition, and intergroup friction. In classic hierarchical structures authority roles are clear. But specialty departments rarely play a superior-subordinate role to one another.

Specialists are less likely than general employees to put the company's good above their own because specialists identify more with their own departments or informal professional groups than with the organization that employs or retains them. This of course provides them with a sense of identity they might otherwise lack, for they rarely consider themselves in the mainstream of line operations. Often held responsible for important contributions to objectives, the specialist does not often feel a sense of ownership. Neither fish nor fowl, often rejected by line operators and not considered a full member of the action team by management, the specialist is often forced to make this identification with the substructures to satisfy his need for security and prestige. They provide a milieu in which he can work out frustrations and hostilities and give him department or professional support. This lends status to his function and reinforces his self-confidence.

Specialty Departments

The majority of the professional specialists whom an organization utilizes work in its departments or other formal divisions. These include purchasing, engineering, quality control, personnel, training, finance, and accounting, among others. Specialized units range in function from the highly intellectual, as is the case with a computer systems group, to the manual or clerical, for example, stores and the mailroom. Most specialty divisions act in service or monitoring capacities to production or other line operations. They can cause intricate intergroup behavior problems.

The Scarcity Principle

Service departments operate around the principle of scarce commodities, partly by necessity and partly by choice. They are in a position to make limited materials or functions even scarcer, thus increasing their stature in the organization by virtue of the control over the supply. In reaction to this a supervisor who realizes that an item of office equipment or production materials is in short supply makes an effort to stockpile for the future, and this drains what little stock is available. He does not consider the impact of his acts on other departments that need the same item.

The greater the specialization in an organization, the less autonomous its departments are likely to be. Thus each unit is dependent upon many others for resources and information. Because almost every department is subject to pressures as the result of its own specialization, tensions mount, not only taking their toll of the department's efficiency but spreading through the organization. The sales staff wants its monthly results from the finance department; production is begging for the new employees it has requested from personnel; and so the pressures climb.

A typical example of how the scarcity principle works is furnished by a typing pool. It is sent memos and reports with special instructions, including the date the copies are needed. Supervisors continue to call the typing pool, wanting their material and indicating the urgency. The typing supervisor responds by telling the callers that she understands the need and is pushing the girls as hard as possible. Her division head investigates a series of complaints and finds that everything sent for typing is marked "Urgent—as soon as possible." Obviously, no priorities can be established by the typing pool supervisor under these circumstances. Pressuring the typists will accomplish nothing except to increase their errors, cause more dissatisfaction, and drive some typists to resign.

Employees in service departments may begin to fight the pressures put upon them by restricting productivity or withholding materials intentionally. Moreover they often have informal agreements, as do production-line workers, not to pressure one another. When possible they may even slow productivity in order to accommodate one another and defend themselves from external as well as internal pressures.

This fighting back is primarily a self-serving reaction, aggressive behavior that gives an outlet to the pressure. It forces the issue on the attention of upper management, which the harassed workers hope will resolve it in some way. If as often happens change does occur, it obviously rewards the aggressive behavior and allows the bottlenecking to go unpunished. This superimposes on the organization another dimension of behavior that serves to complicate—not resolve—basic problems of companywide coordination.

Functional Myopia

While it is understandable that departments should protect their interests, practices like withholding services and hoarding scarce materials do not serve the common good. There are other forms of shortsightedness that are equally harmful to the organization's health.

Specialty departments tend to view their own policies and methods of operation as best for the organization. Consequently each may try to influence company practices through its key executives in order to capture prestige and build its status. This creates friction between line and executive management and between departments.

For example, some finance and accounting people are certified public accountants and subscribe to the standards and procedures that their professional associations support. They sometime have difficulty reconciling their own approaches with those management prefers even though all concerned are ethical and trustworthy.

Specialty departments experience inbreeding of values, goals, and practices. Sometimes a dominant manager will be in a position to impose his style on the organization as a whole. This often blocks agreement between departments and can lead to inefficiency and conflicts throughout the organization.

A specialty department that is insensitive to organizationwide needs causes continuous difficulty. If its monitoring function is too dominant, it can frustrate creative and innovative approaches to work. It can force employees at all levels into a mold and stifle organization renewal. If the monitoring function is too loose, the department cannot justify its existence; the organization may be hampered in its achievement of objectives by error, dishonesty, and sloppy coordination and control.

In all cases the specialty division must be aware of line department commitments. If it is not, the two units may run a collision course. It should harness the tendency to evaluate the good of the organization in terms of its own preferences and to act as though its specialty is singularly important for corporate survival. In brief it must extend its vision and recognize its relationship to the organic system of the organization.

The Management of Specialists

The manager's job is not simplified by surrounding him with specialists, whether they are assemblers performing single, routine functions thousands of times a day or highly trained professionals supporting management in many capacities. Coordination becomes a critical problem; the manager must harmonize the activities of functional units on a comparable horizontal level for which he has no immediate line responsibility with the productive output in his own area of command.

It is one thing to fragment work and hire specialists. It is quite another to insure that the work is integrated—and that people remain on their jobs. Employees may be efficient, stable, and productive; professional specialists may be informative, cooperative, and contributing. But if the work components are not properly coordinated, everyone's efforts are lost.

Coordination is fundamentally a human-oriented skill and not a technological one. Machine A and automated process B can be built to accommodate machine C and process D. Only improper maintenance or perhaps poor process design can alter that relationship. People are not so easily programmed. Technological specialization is predictable; human behavior may not be.

Specialization places the burden on the manager of joining workers and machines, informal subgroups and specialists, organization policies and department procedures into a dynamic entity. Juggling these elements requires broad managerial competence. Some organizations attempt to reduce the complexity of the coordination task by narrowing the manager's span of control. But the manager's function at any level, whether production or executive, cannot be fractioned to the point where he loses self-respect, the loyalty of subordinates, and opportunities to achieve personal need satisfaction.

The span of control that a manager can reasonably handle is problematic. It is not always true that a smaller scope of responsibility means better supervision. Some of the negative aspects of a small span of control are paternalism and a breakdown in formal or traditional department structures, which may be acceptable if the organization environment supports this openness and if the manager is able to maintain effective leadership. Positive aspects are improved worker motivation and closer working relationships between employees and supervisors, which can result in greater involvement in the problem-solving process.

Communication

One of the results of specialization is multiple layers of management. Lapses and distortions occur in the communication process because of the multiple vertical layers as well as the numerous horizontal networks. Yet the manager must maintain open and steady communications even when layers of hierarchy create sizable distance between his people and the information or decision-making sources.

Because lower-ranking managers are remote from the final decision-making level, there are fewer occasions for personal contact. Communication is often in writing. Executives may arrange contacts on the basis of artificial priorities rather than need. Managers down the line thus have longer to wait for responses. Employees who seek approval for change from supervisors lacking the authority to give it become disenchanted with the chain of command and lose confidence in their manager's ability to respond to simple matters. They often see this lag as a lack of interest in them on his part.

The manager's responsibility and need for communication may be further negated by professional specialists, both those working for him and those assigned to monitor his department. It is not uncommon to find communication bypassing vertical organization layers but flowing horizontally. In addition staff advisers usually have access to all executive levels and may short-circuit the chain of command.

Line managers fear and resent the adviser who has the ear of top management. Employees can seek out staff people for counsel or to register complaints. They may get action more quickly than by going to their supervisor, who must work up the chain of command. This tends to block the supervisor and creates suspicion in his mind that advisers and his employees are going around and over him at every turn. Attention to protocol and reinforcing communication with the supervisor can avert unnecessary conflict.

Specialist-Employees

Management generalists are often given responsibility for specialized departments on the assumption that a good manager can manage any function. Some theorists feel that the manager does not need to have expertise as long as he maintains his authority role. But specialist-employees will make demands on him, often because they lack insight into the pressures already imposed upon the leadership position. These demands tend to impinge on his authority, thus creating a condition of confusion and robbing him of satisfactions that are normally inherent in his job.

The manager may lack knowledge in some or all of the specialties for which he is responsible and so be hampered in making independent or innovative decisions. Even with time he may never reach the depth of knowledge that his subordinate specialists have. The people-oriented manager overcomes some of the problem by including key subordinates in the decision-making process, retaining the authority, however, to accept or reject their advice.

The manager who is dependent on specialists in his department sometimes feels a lack of competence even when he has made his authority role clear. Often such a manager experiences postdecision conflict out of a sense of insecurity stemming from his lack of technological expertise. He may harbor resentment against employee-specialists because he fears that they do not respect him and take advantage of his relative ignorance. Further conflict arises when these specialists must be reprimanded or disciplined. Some managers look the other way to prevent employees they are dependent upon from being angry or resigning, although this can cause morale problems among nontechnical employees.

Specialist-Advisers

Specialists have an important intervening and sometimes complicating role when serving as advisers or monitors of a line supervisor or manager. Theoretically the manager has responsibility for overseeing rules, policies, and work standards in his department. But specialists may be assigned to help control and analyze department results. Their advanced techniques make them capable of weighing subtle relationships that the supervisor may be unaware of or lack skill in handling, or have no time to explore.

Some organizations have complex monitoring functions that require careful coordination. If not well-coordinated, signaled with advance notification, and planned so as to involve supervisors and managers in whose area the control is exercised, serious human relations problems can result. Sometimes monitoring functions are performed on an unscheduled or even sporadic basis, which denies all concerned the opportunity to develop workable interpersonal skills.

Practices such as these incline managers to view advisers as "the enemy" rather than as support specialists ready to counsel them on problems before they occur or indicate changes that could avert tieups in weeks or months to come. A common expression that embodies this viewpoint is "corporate cat." It implies all the failings and foibles of a strictly mahogany-row staff member devoid of line practicality and real world orientation. In companies attempting to bridge communication barriers and credibility gaps between administrative and operating managers, efforts are made to bring representatives from both areas into policy-making and problem-solving groups. Some companies using a round-robin employment interviewing technique for middle and upper levels of management also include representatives from the two areas.

Line managers are often restricted from taking specific action without first receiving the approval of experts in the organization. Labor relations and personnel staff may need to be consulted in wage questions and hiring practices, for example, or cost accountants may be involved in inventory and production questions.

Managers rarely want to risk challenging the authority and expertise of advisers the organization has hired. But there may be numerous interpersonal complications. When for example a young, recent business school graduate placed in the role of specialist-adviser puts restraints on an older, school-of-hard-knocks production supervisor, conflict can arise. The latter tends to interpret the advice as a decision or directive. Feeling that his stature has been diminished and hurt that management has seen fit to ignore his practical experience, the supervisor may overreact. If the advice backfires he is likely to blame the specialist while absolving himself by indicating he was only following management's instructions.

Comparable difficulties arise when a staff specialist is called upon for an answer to a line problem he considers complex but the line manager thinks is simple. A good example is the case of an employee who a production supervisor believes is slowing production but whom he is blocked by personnel specialists from firing.

To the supervisor this is idiocy. He has two problems: a production schedule to meet and an employee who is not producing sufficiently. He thus wants to fire the worker in reaction to the hierarchical pressure on his job. But he is also reacting to peer pressure, since other production supervisors expect him to respond to an unproductive employee in a specific way. When he does not he will lose stature in their eyes. But the staff specialists become concerned about inadequate documentation; they want to know how many others on the line produce as much as, more than, or less than the employee in question. If the employee is a member of a minority group, this raises other considerations.

Thwarted in his efforts to rid himself of a "bad" worker, the supervisor typically fumes in frustration, "I've got a product to get out the door and a bummer who won't work! Personnel butts in and makes it a federal case. If they had enough to keep them busy, they wouldn't need to bug me. If I don't meet schedules this month, the boss can shoot personnel for it, not me."

There are many instances when personnel and training specialists advise retaining an employee and trying a different training approach or counseling. A supervisor struggling to meet his monthly production schedule is unlikely to accept the stabilizing role of advisers graciously. He may begin working up the chain of command for relief. He will also be defensive the next time staff specialists offer "advice."

It is a common occurrence for supervisors to quit their jobs because "They kept digging the ground out from under me." This may be the result of too many advisers, each of whom believes his answer is the best. For example, a production problem may be tackled by experts in purchasing, production control, quality control, design, process engineering, personnel, labor relations, and even training. All have different approaches; all have sound ideas; but no one may agree with another or defer to another's judgment on what is the best solution. The supervisor is immobilized, caught in the middle of a technological battle among experts over issues he may not fully understand. All he is aware of is that while the experts are bickering, his department is going down the tubes.

The Added Stress from Specialization

Stress is an unavoidable factor in the work environment, as Chapter 2 discussed. It is present in any group enterprise, no matter how small. But specialization augments the stress load both quantitatively and qualitatively. The causes and the effects on behavior, some of them referred to previously in this chapter, warrant further exploration.

The functional relationships in the modern business have more lateral than hierarchical interdependence. Managers and workers must interact with people who are neither superior nor subordinate in responsibility and many of whom may be providing a service from outside the organization. This means that nearly every employee is dependent in all directions: up to bosses for direction; laterally to peers for support, advice, and coordination; and down to subordinates for output. Dependence on others increases in proportion to the specialization in a company. Employees may rely on the next desk or workbench, another department, or a plant thousands of miles away.

This interdependence heightens both the vertical and the horizontal stress in the work environment by augmenting operations pressure on both planes and social pressure horizontally. When line and peer pressures merge in terms of values and norms of behavior, people tend to work together in a continuum of problem-solving activity. When these two layers are in conflict, they erect barriers to communication, cooperation, and trust.

In this atmosphere employees tend to shirk responsibility for problems. It is relatively easy to pass the buck since so many others are involved. It takes a time-consuming and costly effort to attempt to fix the blame for a routine error or shortage. A kind of blanket reprimand goes out from an upper-level manager, humiliating and arousing frustration in the first-line supervisor. In reaction to this stress, he may rationalize that he did his part and shrug off his managerial responsibility; or he may pass the reprimand broadside to those under him, thus multiplying the stress.

Employees in turn can spend great amounts of time proving their innocence and others' fault in an effort to defend their own interests. This is often a consequence of the low job security that accompanies task specialization—the work is so simple that mistakes are "not allowed" and the employee can be fired almost indiscriminately because a replacement can be trained quickly.

Production groups feel the pressure of demands for shipments at any cost since the customer must be kept happy, even if the unit cost of production exceeds the operation plan. Harsh penalties are threatened for failure to meet schedules, and managers fear for their jobs.

The reward-and-punishment system causes employees to think only of their own survival in the organization. In terms of Maslow's needs hierarchy, the most basic need is threatened.

The stress on workers is also intensified because of the rigidity that surrounds their jobs. They are expected to interact with equipment and other workers in a predictable way based upon what they do and how often. Once that pattern is changed, the employee's behavior changes. Simply the introduction of minor new elements into the work environment tends to modify behavior. New factors on which employees are appraised or even new channels through which written reports and recommendations are funneled can create anxiety and frustration.

Employees must work off the tensions created by stress. They find themselves locked into hopeless situations, facing natural conflicts and predictable breakdowns, but they feel powerless to avert them. Unable to defend themselves against these pressures, some react by adopting a philosophical attitude, trying in effect to alienate themselves from the job and restrain themselves from personal involvement. Other workers become hostile in their homes and vent their pent-up emotions on family members.

Specialization and Organization Renewal

The fragmentation of work and the interdependence that result from specialization slow the process of organization change. Employees do not have the needed diversity and scope of duties in their jobs to feel confident about suggesting companywide changes. Managers, already burdened by time-consuming coordinating tasks, hesitate to involve themselves in efforts that can only complicate their functions further. Moreover recommendations for needed change may be modified to gain the approval and acceptance of other departments or specialties since change of any importance affects many different areas.

These conditions can lead to spectator behavior. Employees watch problems and may comment on their occurrence or ask speculative questions of their superiors. This gives them the satisfaction of having identified a problem and the enrichment of recognition their comments gain while they avoid personal involvement in the decision-making process. Their sense of achievement is thus limited and is gained only through the activities of others.

The hesitancy of employees to undertake change is matched by the slowdown in vertical communications caused by specialization. As organizations grow in size, their complexity increases. This results in additional layers of management for more control. While such growth may seem supportive, it can be destructive. Studies show that in the modern business organization with complex technology, more decisions must be made at the lowest possible level. The lag between need and response increases in geometrical multiples. The result is that opportunities for organization improvement cannot be recovered during or long after the lag.

Specialization to any degree is a double-edged sword that can create doomsday jobs for specialists and for those who rely on them. The challenge is to reap the advantages of specialization without destroying the individual or the organization. Only through enlightened human understanding can this be done. It is not reasonable to expect historic organization relationships to shift radically to meet the challenge of modern specialization. Nor is it reasonable to demand of the specialist rigidity of purpose and inflexibility in his human responses and needs. The answer lies somewhere in between, with the human being as the measure of reason.

FOUR

a study of waste: minority employees

IN RECENT YEARS business has shown increasing concern about people. This is partly the result of government involvement, union activity, and an uncertain economy. Minority relations have become a major concern of government at all levels since the passage of the Civil Rights Act of 1964 and subsequent actions of the Equal Employment Opportunity Commission and the courts.

"Minority relations manager," "equal opportunity coordinator," and other, similar designations are familiar titles in industrial relations departments. Detailed, often computerized statistical analyses of minority hirings and terminations are maintained at considerable cost. Few college recruitment budgets do not include trips to black campuses, and college tuition aid administrators seek out women and ethnic minorities. Sensitivity training for managers is undertaken in many companies. In addition many organizations have community relations projects, donate money to black colleges and social action groups, encourage employees to participate in relevant community programs, support day care centers, and even bus employees to and from work.

Want ads carry the statement "An Equal Opportunity Employer" and add "M or F" in observance of the Equal Pay Act of 1968. Institutional advertisements are run in the minority press and feature pictures and stories about minority members who have made good. Many firms have elected to eliminate preemployment testing rather than untangle the snarl of government directives. Many follow the letter of the law to perfection; photographs of employees are removed from records and are no longer requested on résumés or application blanks. Employment applications have been revised to eliminate references to race, some have eliminated references to sex, and all have been particularly careful about credit and police records. Although it lessens their usefulness, references are given judiciously for fear of legal action.

Few managers anywhere publicly admit to personal feelings of prejudice. They will probably enunciate the company's position on minorities: fair to all, objective, and firmly opposed to any influence of race, religion, national origin, or sex on how applicants and employees are treated. Most firms have policy statements supporting equal rights in employment, promotion opportunities, and pay.

The fact is, however, that discrimination goes on. Company policies have not corrected biased practices. There is strong evidence to show that the gap between what American business says it believes and what it does in the field of minority relations is wide.

For a time it appeared that civil rights legislation and regulatory agencies might cause the traditional occupational imbalances to change. Change has in fact occurred, but it has been woefully inadequate. Blacks even now earn about 46 percent less than whites in most jobs, although some business school graduates have been earning salaries comparable to whites'. While underdevelopment and underutilization of any employee is costly to the employee and the organization, it takes a particularly heavy toll of minority workers, whose jobs are avenues to psychological and social as well as occupational and economic advancement.

A direct measurement of the change in commitment of business executives to civil rights is nearly impossible. But labor population statistics, reflecting opinion turned into action, are an indicator. The best that can be said is that fair treatment of minorities continues to rate a low priority among businessmen.

It would appear therefore that the Civil Rights Act of 1964 has gone the way of the Volstead Act on prohibition, confirming the argument that you cannot legislate morality any more than the weather. The big question is: What happened?

Government Action on Civil Rights

The Bill of Rights, the Declaration of Independence, and the Preamble of the Constitution will remain landmark expressions of the rights of man. The Civil Rights Act of 1964, notwithstanding its congressionalisms and clumsiness, stands alongside these other legislative masterpieces. Dictators and autocrats have for centuries defined the rights men do not have. These documents courageously define the rights men do have.

Antidiscrimination Measures in American History

The early efforts in this country to eradicate legal sanction of discrimination on all grounds—especially racial—were followed by almost a century of legislative retrogression. The tide turned of course with the Civil War and President Abraham Lincoln's Emancipation Proclamation in 1863. In 1883 the Pendleton, or Civil Service, Act became the first federal statute prohibiting religious discrimination. Not for 50 years, until 1933, did sufficient interest mount for other antidiscrimination legislation to pass.

There was considerable discriminatory activity during that period, moreover. States passed laws prohibiting marriages between white and "colored," even indicating the minimum percentage of nonwhite ancestry defining a person's race. In 1896 the United States Supreme Court decided in *Plessy* v. *Ferguson* that legislation is powerless to change in any way "racial distinction as a result of physical differences." The high court summed up: "If one race is inferior to the other socially, the Constitution of the United States cannot put them upon the same plane."

President Franklin D. Roosevelt and the Seventy-third Congress did not agree. In 1933 the unemployment relief act establishing the Civilian Conservation Corps forbade discrimination on the basis of race, color, or creed in government jobs and federally sponsored training programs. The National Industrial Recovery Act set forth a nondiscrimination policy in connection with low-rent federal housing. In 1940 the Ramspeck Act prohibited racial and religious discrimination in civil service jobs and assured equal rights for government employees. President Roosevelt signed Executive Order 8802 in 1941 to establish nondiscrimination as government policy, and Executive Order 9346 in 1943 created the federal government's Fair Employment Practices Committee.

In an effort to rekindle interest in the government's equal rights policies, President Harry S. Truman signed Executive Order 10308 in 1946 requiring some government agencies to include nondiscrimination clauses in agency contracts. Dwight D. Eisenhower created the President's Committee on Government Contracts through Executive Order 10476 in 1953 to reiterate the federal position on equal rights.

But all these executive orders had the weakness of including no enforcement provisions. The government bodies concerned could recommend, argue, and attempt to influence, but they could do no more. The Eisenhower committee, however, differed somewhat from the others in that its findings went on public record.

The first and possibly most dramatic act of equal rights enforcement in the twentieth century occurred n 1957, when President Eisenhower sent troops to Little Rock, Arkansas, to defend the school desegregation principle enunciated in the Supreme Court's 1954 decision on *Brown* v. *Board of Education of Topeka*. From that point on there was growing concern about civil rights. In 1961 President John F. Kennedy issued Executive Order 10925 establishing the Equal Employment Opportunity Commission. For the first time equal rights in employment were required in the private sector for recipients of government contracts.

Three years later, following Kennedy's assassination and during the administration of President Lyndon B. Johnson, Congress passed the Civil Rights Act of 1964 after tortuous maneuvering, compromise, and brilliant strategizing. It has become one of the most significant pieces of social legislation in the nation's history.

Employment Provisions of the Civil Rights Act

Title VII of the Civil Rights Act of 1964 deals with equal employment opportunity. It states that race, color, creed, religion, and national origin (and suggests sex and age as well) are not relevant to employment qualifications or working conditions after employment. The law covers employers, employment agencies, unions, and joint management and union committees. The act lists what cannot be done, such as barring employment, restricting promotions, and using differential pay scales. But it is silent on what is to be done. Section 703(j) of Title VII attempts to assure that the act does not intend to correct racial imbalance in employment resulting from discrimination. Section 708 insures states' rights by affirming that Title VII exempts no one from obeying state laws unless these are contrary to the terms of Title VII.

Controversy raged over the act and early pronouncements of the Equal Employment Opportunity Commission. Even the most obscure provisions of the law were argued. In *Dobbins* v. *Local 212*, a labor arbitration case argued before the United States District Court of Southern Ohio in 1969, the court denied that the Civil Rights Act of 1964 requires affirmative action and rejected the idea that preferential treatment of minorities is lawful. The act indeed does not require affirmative action, just as it does not require correction of imbalances. President Johnson's Executive Orders 11246 and 11375 in 1965–1966 provided for affirmative action but only on the part of government contractors. In the years since, the Equal Employment Opportunity Commission has gained growing enforcement authority, and greater attention has been focused on sex discrimination.

Reactions in the Business Community

The shock waves created by the Civil Rights Act of 1964 continue to reverberate through the business community. Companies that have felt a sense of obligation toward minorities have exercised it in charitable activities. Government action has brought the question of treatment of minorities into the realm of business. Companies have reacted in various ways, ranging from continued discriminatory practices to efforts to reverse past and present wrongs.

Discriminatory Policies

The most blatant form of job discrimination is of course a flat refusal even to consider minority-group members for employment. Companies find many reasons to justify this position. Some professional organizations—architecture firms, stock brokerages, advertising agencies—argue that many of their clients do not want to deal with minority-group members. In addition, they say, they utilize such traditionally discriminatory places as athletic clubs and private country clubs for business occasions; thus it would be awkward if minority members represented the firm. Their final argument is that few minority people have sufficient experience in their professional specialties to qualify for employment. There is probably some validity to this last argument. Minorities have traditionally not pursued certain occupations because employment has not been available to them. The flaw in the argument is that it disregards cause and effect: it is the long history of discrimination in employment that has discouraged minority candidates from preparing for these professions.

Other businesses are highly ambivalent. They vow that discrimination is not sanctioned, and they hold to the letter of job qualification prerequisites. If minority-group members happen to apply for employment, they are treated with courtesy, are allowed to complete employment applications, and may even be interviewed. However, they will be hired only if white applicants who are "roughly as qualified" are unavailable at the time. Promotion opportunities are generally unavailable to minority employees in these companies, and pay rates are often different for minorities and whites. Few minorities are attracted to such firms, and those who are rarely bring legal action against them.

Color-blind Policies

Managers with the authority to recruit, hire, and promote and who feel a corporate and personal sense of obligation toward minorities may also fear adverse management and public reaction. Thus they will remain "color-blind"; that is, they take a neutral position. They will not discriminate, but on the other hand they believe that bending backward for blacks or other minorities is discriminatory against whites.

The main policy of such firms is to hire "enough" minority candidates to keep within the letter of the law, and they involve themselves in detailed record keeping to maintain that "enough." They of course must avoid government contracts, and through their internal policies and external public relations, they make an attempt to create sufficient uncertainty about their practices to reduce the risk of legal involvement.

However, a number of these companies have been defendants in civil rights suits brought about by minority employees. The problem is that the backlog of discrimination charges filed with the Equal Employment Opportunity Commission will not be cleared for years. The commission takes action against offenders, but the number of investigations is insufficient to blanket the country, and the number of such companies is very high. The result is little change, and the overall impact of both government action and public sentiment becomes minimal.

Active Antidiscrimination Policies

A growing number of business organizations challenge the argument that affirmative action on behalf of minorities is a form of discrimination since it gives minorities breaks that majority employees do not get. Companies with antidiscrimination policies contend that affirmative action is morally and financially sound because it helps correct injustice and provides the means by which entire future generations will become consumers.

Some of these businesses were openly involved in civil rights issues long before it became popular or mandatory to be so. Many of them were not even government contractors. They have formed alliances with other firms to provide training for minorities and guaranteed job placement. Management ranks have been opened to minority-group members and active steps have been taken to seek out, attract, and hire them.

A few examples will illustrate how some companies implement affirmative action as an approach to developing and retaining minorities. Some organizations select minority applicants who meet the minimum requirements of the job; some will hire minorities even though more qualified white applicants are available. They do this on the assumption that the qualified white has many more opportunities for employment than the minority candidate. On the basis of indications (or actual evidence) that job prerequisites are overstated, some organizations lower their minimum requirements in order to increase the salary level and strengthen the employee's buying power in the labor market. They eliminate artificial requirements in many ways: by lowering the stipulations concerning education level and previous experience; by validating employment tests with minority groups in order to correct cultural or class biases in favor of the majority population; by training personnel staff members to discard subliminal prejudices against superficial differences from the "norm" in dress or speech patterns.

Many of these firms reach into minority communities to work against the effects of underprivilege. Some build branch offices in ghetto areas and staff these locations with neighborhood residents. Others participate in urban renewal and community affairs activities and provide scholarships for minority youngsters.

Obviously there are business as well as ethical motives behind the affirmative action programs of many organizations. Some respond in this manner because they are too large not to. Their goods and services touch millions of lives, and many fear public resentment if they fail to respond. They want to avoid the economic pinch and bad publicity of a minority boycott. They also realize that allowing generation after generation of nonconsumers to build up in the economy is bad for business in the long run.

This is not to say that these organizations do not sincerely believe in the civil rights movement; the degree of their involvement shows their moral commitment. Unlike color-blind companies, they do not think that rigorous impartiality in hiring, placement, promotions, and pay will produce an integrated workforce. They argue that affirmative action is ultimately the only way integration can be effected. Both theory and practice seem to side with them. The difference between color blindness and affirmative action is the key to eliminating doomsday jobs for minorities and helping reduce high minority turnover.

Reactions in Minority Communities

If there is ambivalence in the business community, there is confusion, even conflict, among minority-group members. There is little agreement even on who the leaders are. The voices that are heard by the masses are rarely moderate. The young are torn: whether to become a "Thank you, Mr. Bossman" sellout, an independent who demands his rights—and may find himself unemployed as a result—or a color-blind conformist groping for identity in the white corporate world.

Moderate social action organizations do what they can to train applicants, make referrals, and meet color-blind business on its own ground. They work quietly within the constraints of traditional business attitudes, and many are effective in surmounting the obstacles against their members. They often work to prevent discrimination complaints from going into litigation, acting in the role of conciliators and mediators.

Militants, however, accuse them of Uncle Tomism or its equivalents in other minority groups—gringoism, male-chauvinist defeatism, and the like. Militant groups seek action now; they want immediate and dramatic reform in conservative American industry. Some theorists and black leaders, for example, argue that black economic nationalism may be the ultimate solution to social inequities. They insist that the alienated black can achieve equality only if the black community achieves the economic and political base needed to unify it. Short of this they see continued racial strife.

Some minority leaders insist that discrimination in employment could be eliminated quickly and for all time if establishment executives and those who control the massive economy of industry decided to institute change. They point out that there simply has not been a transfer of skills and authority to minority employees. This can be equated ultimately to a transfer of power from one group to another. Historically majority groups hesitate to give up or share their positions of power. Many minority leaders believe that equal employment opportunity laws and appeals to heart and mind have not produced sufficient change and cannot be expected to. The disproportionate representation of minorities in the nation's workforce substantiates this argument.

Barriers to Minority Employment

Members of ethnic minority groups who find it difficult or impossible to gain a foothold in the white employment world are often blocked because their subcultures are perceived as being incompatible with the majority culture. The continuing alienation of millions of people raises both moral and practical questions.

The employment patterns of minority workers are different from those of the rest of the workforce because the uncertainty of jobs affects life styles. Some minorities have no permanent address. They live close to their place of employment and are ready to move where there is work. Rarely developing the neighborhood ties characteristic of the white middle class and having few possessions, they are mobile. Reference checking of minority applicants may reveal arrests (few convictions), which are often a reflection of community law-enforcement practices.

The pattern of employment is self-perpetuating because simple survival demands all the resources many minority workers have. They may be financially unable to allow their children to complete secondary education, much less attend college. Some of the young people do not desire education. There is not a tradition of books or schooling in their families. Education requirements for jobs tend to reinforce racial barriers since it is true that there are fewer minority-group graduates from high school, junior college, and college than whites.

As pointed out before, minorities have generally avoided learning certain skills because their chances for employment that would utilize those skills are slight. As a result they lack experience and training for certain jobs and can rarely qualify where inflexible prerequisites are established. Thus they find themselves in a vicious circle: They lack experience and preparation and cannot qualify for jobs that can provide these. Some companies will give minority-group applicants only jobs they are clearly qualified to perform, which usually means lower-level positions in which enrichment, development, and advancement potential are slight or nonexistent.

Language usage is a barrier to employment for members of numerous minority groups. The foreign-born worker whose command of English is not yet strong faces a major obstacle. Even the American-born, however, may find that his speech patterns weigh against him. Many interviewers and managers insist they have trouble understanding minority "dialects." In addition an applicant may use colloquialisms that are part of the vocabulary of the ghetto. These expressions are sometimes interpreted as disrespectful and may cause a supervisor to comment to personnel, "You don't really think I'm going to bring someone into my department who is likely to close a telephone conversation with 'Right on'!"

Good credit, for so long among the pillars of middle-class virtue, is not easily eliminated as an employment and placement criterion even though it is largely unmeasurable and perhaps irrelevant. Laws regulating credit verification notwithstanding, interviewers form "impressions" about credit and indebtedness and often equate these factors with instability on the job. Minority applicants also often fail to meet other unwritten standards of stability—ownership of cars and homes, maintenance of bank accounts, and similar signs of a "proper" work ethic. Thus when they do go for employment interviews, the cards are stacked against them.

Traditional Hiring Practices

Personnel staff members and interviewers in factories and offices continue to practice selective forms of discrimination. Many employment departments require disproportionate experience of minority applicants, hiring them only if their qualifications far exceed the acceptable minimum, as if overqualification were a way to protect white interests. Companies seem somehow proud when they hire overqualified minority candidates. Conversely they are skeptical and even defensive about those who "get by" with only the minimum requirements, although they typically allow whites to do so.

Employment applications and tests frequently disconcert or intimidate minority candidates. New laws regulating questions that can be included on employment application forms have brought some relief. But job placement analysts function in habitual ways. They are not likely to give up "tried and true" questions long used on the forms. Similarly employment tests take on a venerable patina and are difficult to challenge, even though they may contain patent biases against members of subcultures because they are based on the norms of the white middle-class community.

The interviewing process itself is often demeaning to the minority candidate. This also is a result of habitual interview patterns and problem-solving styles on the part of employment office staff and managers who are unwilling to modify approaches with which they feel secure. They know too that the interview function lacks measurable objectivity and that high levels of chance are inherent in it. They evaluate an applicant's personal and occupation history by using themselves as the norm, relying on white middle-class virtues and standards. The evaluation often becomes a generalized critical social appraisal. Interviewers tend to look for applicant characteristics that are very much like their own, and most are repelled by dissimilarities.

Interviewers convey their conviction of the minority candidate's inferiority by both what they say and what they leave unsaid. The rules of work are reiterated in detail. All the reasons someone can get fired are revealed, and admonitions are given about drinking and "fooling around." But often very little attention is paid to explaining the importance of the job and the part it plays in the total production process. Few supervisors make efforts to motivate, stimulate, or educate at the time of the interview even where white applicants are concerned. Efforts to arouse a minority applicant's interest, evaluate his needs, and prepare him in a way that builds toward a more productive relationship after employment are even slighter and less effective.

Because applicants' capabilities are not properly assessed or utilized, the jobs they are given if they are selected for employment often have doomsday dimensions for them. Rapid learning curves, lack of enrichment and development, and boredom foster a high absentee rate, tardiness, and finally turnover, perhaps followed by employment elsewhere on another doomsday job.

As long as minority candidates are treated like dull-witted children who are devoid of values and unwilling or unable to act responsibly except under threats to their fundamental security, equal employment opportunity pledges and mottos are worthless.

From the Other Side of the Desk

Sometimes a minority applicant can be placed in a doomsday job because of an honest misinterpretation of the information he presents. In an effort to sidestep the disappointment and humiliation of being found underqualified, candidates may deliberately apply for low-paying jobs beneath their skill level. Often this is an effort to increase their chances of getting jobs and avoid open competition with white applicants, in which the minority candidate usually loses. But this strategy is rarely effective. On the one hand it contradicts the stereotype of the aggressive, pushy militant. On the other it reinforces the equally invalid stereotype of the lazy worker who lacks ambition and initiative.

Applicant bias may also skew the picture a minority-group member presents of himself. This is a defense mechanism through which the applicant, especially for a management job, protects himself from the ambiguities of the selection process he perceives as threatening to him and his self-concept. The object of the bias is the employment interviewer, whom the candidate perceives as being unqualified to assess him properly because of a lack of either expertise in a technical area or social awareness. These applicants want more personalized treatment during the interview and on the job because they see themselves as being atypical of the minority group.

An example is a black professional applicant whose education and training are like those of whites but whose life style is dissimilar. He may feel frustrated and angry when asked questions about his background and current circumstances. The questions seem either leading or simplistic, intended to belittle or snare, and to avoid the bigger issues about which he is concerned.

The strategy this applicant adopts is to appeal to the interviewer's mind. He feels the need to educate and enlighten the interviewer about circumstances in his life and in his world. His answers to questions are therefore not always direct and to the point. He may preface them with a commentary, introduced by an "As you probably know . . ." or "I'm sure you understand that. . . ."

The interviewer may lose patience and begin to use closed questions that restrict answers to "Yes" or "No" in an effort to block this kind of elaboration. Not only is this frustrating to the applicant; it forces him to hesitate, and it can even make him appear evasive. He may avoid the question in its original form, restate it, and proceed with his own interpretation of it. The interviewer listens and responds, "But you still haven't answered my question." The defeated applicant may surrender with "I'm sorry; I can't."

Job placement may be denied because of the applicant's seeming evasiveness. If he is hired, the job assignment may be heavily influenced by the interviewer's evaluation that although he is educated and qualified, he has difficulty expressing himself or is so vague he may have something to hide. This could open the door to a doomsday job for which the applicant is clearly overqualified and knows it. The result is frustration and turnover.

Traditional On-the-Job Practices

From the first day of work on, the expectations of the supervisor and the minority employee are low; and their contacts with each other are likely to be guarded at best. The relationship begins with mistrust and often deteriorates from there.

Job content is notoriously deficient, as previous sections pointed out. Many minority employees find little motivation or opportunity for development in their work. The salary is typically low, and they can get monotonous, low-paying drudgery anywhere. Worse, many see their jobs as hopeless, never-changing boredom and even enslavement. They watch as others are promoted and advanced in salary while they experience tokenism. Not surprisingly turnover is very high.

The turnover rate has other causes as well. One is that minorities are more likely to be fired as a disciplinary measure than are whites. A minority worker failing in his job may not consider this to be a punishable act. He may argue that punishment will not help him since the poor performance is not willful. The logic of this argument holds for the many minority employees who need more training and more time to gain skills. Another worker may lack the experience to see the seriousness of persistent tardiness or absenteeism. This is not an argument against using disciplinary action if needed in such a case. The point is that disciplinary action needs to be weighed against the offender's general background and previous experience.

Job stability is tenuous at best for the mass of minority workers. With the advent of automation some years back, one of the great fears was unemployment. While automation did not bring unemployment for semiskilled and skilled workers or significantly reduce the total number of people any company employed, it did foreclose a great many unskilled jobs in factories and offices, and it is largely unskilled jobs that minority workers hold. Companies were faced with hard decisions about whom to fire, whom to lay off, and whom to retain. When there were borderline cases, most companies chose to retain more whites than minorities.

Minority unemployment continues to reflect the weak defense

minorities have against changing times. Management development programs, skills training, and promotion to jobs offering occupational visibility were for years entirely closed to many minorities. Although the entrance of minority employees into these areas has increased, it remains minimal.

Performance Appraisals

Minority applicants and employees eligible for promotion are sometimes placed in doomsday jobs because interviewers and managers have difficulty interpreting the prior successes and failures of these workers. Interviewers fear taking the risk of promoting minorities into "better" jobs because they are unable to understand the implications of a minority person's record of successive failure. It is hard enough to assess the performance—particularly poor performance—of white employees and applicants; the problem is compounded for minorities because of cultural differences and bias.

Anxiety is an important factor in minority screening. Minority workers more often than white tend to perceive the work milieu as threatening and ambiguous. A high-anxiety employee who has often experienced failure may demonstrate low performance because of feelings of fear and the desire to avoid failure-producing situations. Managers should take into account psychological evidence of the effects of failure in evaluating past performance.

Typically white interviewers and managers do not understand the symbols of success that have value and importance in the minority community. The minority employee whose ultimate symbol of success may not be money (beyond that required to satisfy physiological needs) is likely to view employment security and stability as achievements while the interviewer takes a rather ho-hum view of these. Often minority employees do not hold jobs that provide visible evidence of success according to middle-class definitions. The jobs are usually routine, junior-level positions at most, in which performance is based on ability to meet rigid minimum standards. Often performance appraisal systems evaluate achievement strictly on the basis of these minimum standards. It is not uncommon for there to be no formal appraisal, so that the only record of performance lies in the memory or subjective judgment of a former superior.

There are exceptions to the record of poor employment practices of course in all lines of business and in all kinds of jobs and professions. But these exceptional employment situations do not come about by accident. Fair and unbiased treatment of minorities is most often the result of total commitment, usually on the part of a few people at the top of the corporate hierarchy who effect change through authority and personal persuasion. They recognize that it is not only unenlightened but unproductive to attempt motivating only part of a workforce, wasting the human resources of the rest in doomsday jobs.

Age and Sex Discrimination

The Equal Pay Act and the Age Discrimination Act of 1967 attempted to do for women and those between 40 and 65 years of age what the Civil Rights Act attempted to do for minorities in general. These laws, however, neither proposed nor urged special treatment for the two categories of people involved. They simply made it illegal—because it is unreasonable—to judge ability, potential, and effectiveness on the basis of sex or age. What has been said thus far about ethnic minorities applies as well to women and the 40–65 age bracket.

Women have long experienced humiliation and frustration in efforts to achieve the occupation status so many of them deserve. They have by and large been thwarted in their attempts to rise in or even join the ranks of practicing professions. The myths about why women cannot assume managerial roles are many and as invalid as myths about male managers. But the big lie is a potent adversary.

Over the years the jobs for which women could qualify have been of little stature—simplified, overcontrolled, and deprived of avenues for development. Male college graduates have been selected for management trainee positions almost to the exclusion of females. As a result well-educated women have been constrained to work as secondary-school teachers, secretaries, and salespeople. The waste has been phenomenal. Intelligent women with ability and background have been straitjacketed into doomsday jobs while the myths have proliferated about their instabilities and personality limitations. The vicious circle continues to turn for them as it does for ethnic minorities.

The problem facing the older worker, particularly one who must seek a new job when he is beyond 40, differs from that of other minorities only in timing. This classification of employees—assuming membership in the white middle class, of course—loses favor with American business simply by dint of age.

Business argues that "oldsters" 40 to 65 years old and more are slow to learn, cannot shake the lessons of the past, can be expected to have failing eyesight and to tire quickly, and are difficult to motivate because they do not relate well to new ideas. Yet there is rather persuasive evidence that the older worker still qualifies for high-risk, high-payoff, important positions: *Most top executives today are themselves in the*

40-to-65-year-old age group. If older workers do indeed learn more slowly, they tend to remain on the job longer than their younger counterparts. Their learning curves may be less dramatic, but the jobs on which they are employed will not turn over two, three, and even four times a year.

When willing older workers are placed in doomsday jobs, the organization loses valuable opportunities to bolster unstable work groups and avail itself of maturity and experience. This age group has an undisputed record of stability, loyalty, and established skills and maintains a better attendance record than the 18- to 35-year-olds, despite the fact that energy and health wane with age.

Disregarding the advantages of retaining older workers, American industry continues the pattern of pursuing employees aged 18 to 35 though they have proved to be the most volatile, highest-risk, most restless cut of worker. The 40- to 65-year-olds continue to face hard times in the job market.

In terms of sheer numbers, moreover, it would serve business well to turn its focus on the older age group. The 15- to 25-year-olds are the fastest-growing age group in America. The group 35 to 44 is our slowest-growing. These are the people who now supply business with its skilled technicians and middle managers. The 45- to 55-year-olds are showing no increase in numbers, but the over-55 group is the most rapidly increasing of the adult generations.

The effect of rejection on older workers is destructive. Most react with hopelessness. Many become embittered because employers see no future in them. Older workers want to be challenged and stimulated; their human needs do not dissipate with age. The aging process accelerates when a person recognizes that he is no longer a contributing member of society.

From the standpoint of practicalities, the reduction (not total loss) of powers experienced by people in their 60s and even beyond does put business in a quandary. The way out of this quandary may well be found in an aspect of organization functioning that with other age groups tends to create doomsday jobs: specialization. The simplified jobs in the highly mechanized and automated world of American business provide an excellent place for the older worker with diminished capabilities. Certainly the miniaturized technology of many industries would seem an employment haven for thousands still able and willing to work.

Business bears a terrible burden when it decides the fate of women and older workers. In the past it was relatively easy for companies to relegate human beings to doomsday jobs. Because of insensitivity and belief in myths, they saw no relationship between inequitable practices and turnover. Today this shortsightedness has cleared somewhat with minorities and women but is still routine with older workers. Business must question whether the cost is worth the waste.

Pledges Must Be Implemented

There is good reason to believe that the gains made in civil rights might never have happened had there not been laws forcing attention to a critical social and moral problem. The theory operating here is that forced behavior may become willing behavior and that the law will reflect and become a part of the social value system. With experience and over time, fear of unknowns subsides.

Business organizations by and large have needed the force of law to make them aware of discrimination in employment practices. Some, struck by the truth in the law, have undertaken corrective action on a broad scale. Others, slower to perceive the vital link between the welfare of society and their own, have only made pledges to obey the letter of the law.

But a pledge of equal employment opportunity does not effect change. It has no meaning until it is applied by purposeful human action. Social accountability aside, fair treatment of all employees benefits the organization; discrimination hurts its interests. Unwillingness to provide development and achievement opportunities to every worker results in costly underutilization of manpower now and in the future. The company that fails to see each employee at every level in the hierarchy as in training for increasing use of his potential must be willing to write off the future loss of a given percentage of its manpower and its profits. If there is enough of this capping off of people and a sizable portion of employees becomes either unpromotable or incapable of responding to the growth needs of the job, the total organization potential is drastically weakened.

There is a broader perspective as well that businesses, as major component units of society at large, have an obligation to keep in mind. Common sense dictates what history has shown: Civilized society is not preserved when the authority of law is ignored. The truth inherent in just law has a lasting and pragmatic quality, and the wisdom of the law is realized in a society in which all men willingly fall heir to its gifts as well as its penalties and have the freedom and challenge to right the wrongs they have created.

FIVE

turnover costs can be measured

TURNOVER costs American business billions of dollars a year. It is the most costly and least understood of all phenomena working against productivity, efficiency, and ultimately profits.

Business analyzes turnover costs only in terms of actual expenses associated with terminations: various forms of severance pay, excess unemployment insurance, recruitment costs or agency fees, travel and moving costs, and the like. These figures, often staggering, are incomplete because calculations of production losses and capital equipment down time for the period between employment and termination are not included; nor are extra costs of replacement, such as a higher salary level.

Business has not yet been motivated to devise reliable methods of assessing the costs of losing its human resources for several reasons. One is that turnover figures are not made part of the profit and loss statement. Another is that they are generally not included in the mainstream of management data on which managerial performance is based. Moreover turnover information is usually so insufficient that the business organization has difficulty getting a handle on the problem. And because executives traditionally demand "real" numbers and facts for problem solving and decision making, creative efforts to explore the question of turnover are generally stifled.

The dollar cost of equipment down time can be measured more precisely than that of a lost employee and is certain to generate more immediate executive concern. All expenditures associated with equipment—depreciation and maintenance and repair costs, for example—can be easily calculated by accountants. In addition it is impossible to pretend that these costs do not exist. The loss of human resources cannot be costed so readily; nor is executive concern about it nearly so acute. Few if any companies have yet held themselves accountable for the depreciation of human resources.

Yet computing a company's turnover costs need not be a complex venture. If well-planned the cost study produces tangible results in a short time. The major requirement is to decide what factors to analyze. If some factors are unavailable or costly to obtain, they should be estimated, at least in the early stages of the study. Known criteria can be used to formulate the estimates. A few standardized estimates in an array of good, hard numbers can be as effective as wholly substantiated findings in attracting management's attention and eliciting its commitment to resolving the turnover problem.

Some Guidelines for Measuring Turnover

Many studies have attempted to establish reasonably sized rates and cost elements of turnover. Some studies provide formulas; others provide only listings based upon job titles. Differences in estimates are as staggering as the amounts of turnover and the costs they describe. These differences are due to variations in type and size of business, geographic location, management styles and policies, anticipated growth potential of companies, usual length of employees' service, training costs, administrative overhead, and many other factors.

No company should strive to eliminate turnover completely because incompetent and unwilling workers will accumulate over time and will deter the company from reaching objectives. Typically a turnover rate of from 20 to 25 percent for clerical or white-collar workers is acceptable while in some manufacturing fields a rate of as high as 35 to 40 percent may be acceptable.

From a purely economic standpoint, it usually costs more to terminate an employee than to hire one. A general rule of thumb puts involuntary termination costs at about 2½ to 3½ times the cost of recruitment and hiring. Some conservative midpoint estimates of overall cost figures can be given. A firm of 200 employees with a monthly turnover rate of about 2 percent will average $20,000 to $25,000 a year in costs; training a salesman will run about $7,000; a clerical employee can account for $350 to $500 in turnover costs; replacing the average exempt worker ranges from $2,500 to $4,000 annually.

The most reliable cost estimates are those a company develops for itself. To do this it must first discover how much turnover it is experiencing. Using these data it can then construct a cost analysis program to measure the inroads that turnover is making into company earnings. Turnover costs can be divided into two major catagories: (1) tangible costs, which can be measured, and (2) intangible costs, which are difficult or impractical to measure. It is usually enough to know that intangible costs, even though incalculable, are at work in the system chipping away at profits.

Framing the Problem Statistically

Traditional definitions of turnover are nothing more than verbal descriptions of how turnover is calculated. Statistical methods are available that offer more analytical capabilities.

Companywide Analysis

The first step in calculating the size of turnover is to compute how much loss the company as a whole is experiencing. The basic figures needed are the number of employees leaving and the on-roll count, or number remaining, each month. (There are a number of other ways to compute the base for the calculation of turnover figures. The federal turnover reports use the employee census at the pay period nearest to the middle of the month. Others use the average of the employment level at the beginning and end of the month as the base. Most companies calculate turnover as described here.) The severance figure should include voluntary and involuntary terminations: quits, retirements, discharges, and layoffs. The on-roll count can be the average during the month or the number at the end of the month. Dividing the termination figure by the on-roll count and multiplying the quotient by 100 gives the turnover rate:

$$\frac{\text{Number of terminations}}{\text{On-roll count}} \times 100 = \text{Turnover rate}$$

The anticipated monthly figure times 12 provides a broad indicator of the annual percentage of turnover if the current circumstances remain constant. Fluctuations can be observed, and these should be related to known changes within or outside the organization. Turnover may increase during periods of accelerated hiring, at the end of a school year, when new methods are introduced into the production process, or when changes in normal routines occur. It may decrease toward the end of the calendar year, when hiring is slower, during the introduction of training and development programs, or in periods of relative stability in production and administrative processes. The rates should be compared with those of other companies in the same geographic area and industry to determine similarities and differences and to test basic assumptions about the causes of turnover.

Once it has determined its turnover rate, a company can gain further insight into its employment structure by calculating its worker replacement rate. First it determines its monthly expansion, or accession, rate:

$$\frac{\text{Number of hires}}{\text{On-roll count}} \times 100 = \text{Expansion rate}$$

The replacement rate is the expansion or turnover rate, whichever is smaller.

If the replacement rate is negative (that is, if the separation rate exceeds the accession rate) when the company is in a hiring mode and the labor market is ample, someone in the employment function has fallen asleep at the switch; under such circumstances the two rates should be similar. When a company in a hiring mode finds it has a decreasing replacement rate, this is more alarming than during a period of cutback. At a time when attrition is desirable, a positive or increasing replacement rate indicates an unfavorable situation.

Additional turnover calculations can isolate problems. A company may find it valuable to compare voluntary with involuntary termination rates. Layoffs, which often run their course without analysis, can be rich in data. Analyzing the layoff rate of those with long experience or high technological skill provides a clue to some of the causative factors of the layoff.

Department Analysis

The next step in framing the turnover problem is to determine the rate for each major department or location in the company. The same formula, number of terminations divided by on-roll count and multiplied by 100, is used, and each reporting unit should submit not only its overall turnover rate but an analysis by job title and grade.

It is also advisable to include in department rates the number of employees transferred from one department to another. Transfers mean a series of promotions, reassignments, or upgradings. Transfers are beneficial over the long run to the company and the employees and have a positive effect on the overall turnover rate, but they do create the need for retraining, reorientation, and the restructuring of once-efficient work teams, all of which can cause temporary reductions of productivity.

When a department loses an employee because of a transfer, it must absorb the loss. Upgrading an employee already knowledgeable about most aspects of the job and the department helps reduce training time, creates less disruption of normal routine, and is less costly than bringing in someone new. But someone must take the place of the upgraded employee. A chain reaction can be set off that touches many departments. Unless jobs are being closed out, a new hire may be brought in at some point, preferably at the lowest possible grade, after the transfer and promotion chain reaction is completed. These changes must be accounted for when turnover is being costed because most if not all of the cost factors to be explained on the following pages may be present.

There are many ways of analyzing and utilizing department turnover figures. A few approaches are as follows:

1. Rank departments from highest to lowest in turnover rate each month, and note the repeaters.
2. Relate turnover rates to hiring activity to see what effect accelerated hiring has on turnover.
3. Determine what changes in normal routine took place during the month or earlier that may have contributed to the turnover.
4. Find out which department rates fluctuate similarly to that of the total company. These may become forecast indicators.
5. Determine what portion of the turnover rate reflects transfers and promotions.

6. Determine which departments supply and which receive promotable or transferable people and with what frequency.
7. Project an annual turnover rate. This will provide a clue to possible hiring and training needs and some indication of cost.

Tangible Cost Factors

Tangible costs, as noted earlier, are measurable; intangible in the main are not. Tangible costs are usually high enough to make a considerable impression. They include employment expenses, breaking-in costs, startup costs, training costs, separation expenses, short-timer costs, social security tax payments, and unemployment insurance contributions.

Employment expenses. These include all direct and indirect costs associated with hiring. Some theorists maintain that only employment costs associated with separations and replacements should be calculated since even a company with no turnover adds people because of expansion and a company must maintain the employment function regardless. The cost schedule as conceived of here, however, charges the entire employment function to turnover, whether employment activity is related to internal expansion or replacement. The function is then prorated among hires, reinstatements, and rehires.

1. Advertising expense for recruitment purposes.
2. Printing charges for company publications such as benefit booklets.
3. Agency fees.
4. Search fees.
5. Costs of selection or prescreening, including physical examination, testing, and reference checking.
6. Travel costs of candidates.
7. Travel costs of recruiters.
8. Wages and salaries of employees whose primary responsibility is in the employment function.
9. A reasonable proportion of wages and salaries of employees who spend only part of their time in the employment process.
10. Wages and salaries of those involved in the interview process and in subsequent directly related meetings or decision-making conferences.
11. An allocation of office supply costs.
12. An allocation of normal overhead expenses.

Breaking-in costs. This factor consists of all expenses for supervisory and nonsupervisory personnel in connection with on-the-job training of a new employee. Breaking-in costs can range from $125 to $200 for the average clerical, technical, or hourly production worker and are $350 to $375 for the average salaried nonexempt employee.

1. Wages and salaries of supervisors and key nonsupervisory personnel engaged in on-the-job training.
2. The cost of materials and equipment directly associated with on-the-job training.
3. The cost of the production time lost by a nonsupervisory trainer from his usual responsibilities.
4. Wages and salaries of people maintaining learning curve statistics and other associated record keeping.
5. Wages and salaries of those developing materials to be used in on-the-job training if other than the supervisor.

Startup costs. These are the costs of substandard work performed by a new employee. For production workers a conservative estimate is $330, for salaried nonexempt employees about $650, and for clerical and technical employees about $250. Startup costs continue until the employee's productivity reaches the average employee output for the same job.

Training costs. These include formal classroom training expenses, not on-the-job training, which is usually accounted for under breaking-in costs.

1. Wages and salaries of training personnel.
2. The cost of materials and supplies used in the training classes.
3. Normal overhead expenses prorated among the number of people trained.
4. The cost of orientation and tours.
5. The cost of special seminars held away from the place of work for training and development.
6. Tuition aid and reimbursement for education outlays.
7. The cost of renewal programs such as cycling sales training and technological updating courses.
8. Costs associated with retraining transferred or promoted employees who subsequently leave.
9. Miscellaneous expenditures—on name tags, refreshments, photographs, and so forth.

Separation expenses. They include costs incurred as a direct result of an employee's separation from the company. On the average the expenses run approximately $200 for a production worker, nearly $300 for an office or technical worker, and a bare minimum of $600 for exempt personnel.

1. The cost of production lost during recruitment for a replacement.
2. The cost of productive equipment down time.

3. Wages and salaries of all personnel working on the separation, including employees carrying out exit interviewing, terminal processing, and payroll and credit union record keeping.
4. Severance pay.

Short-timer costs. These costs are quite difficult to measure; an estimate may be all that is possible. However, it is worth the effort to isolate them. They include all costs attributable to the behavior of employees who plan to quit.

1. The cost of the employee's reduced productivity.
2. The cost of the reduced productivity of fellow workers due to time spent with the terminating employee in conversation and farewell.
3. The cost of the employee's time away from work for job hunting.
4. The cost of the employee's time spent writing résumés and using company facilities to reproduce and mail them.

Social security tax payments. A company must bear the cost of an additional FICA tax contribution as a result of turnover. Currently employers pay social security taxes on half of the first $10,800 of each employee's annual earnings. If the annual pay for a given job is greater than $10,800 and more than one worker fills that job during the year, then the company incurs a tax liability on half of all the amount above $10,000 paid for the job.[1] Of course if the ceiling on the taxable pay is raised, this reduces the added turnover expense.

Unemployment insurance contributions. The federal and state unemployment insurance ceiling for earnings in a calendar year is $4,200.[2] When this ceiling has been reached, employers cease to make contributions just as in the case of social security taxes. Turnover results in continued employer contributions past the point where they are expected to stop for each job.

Pay versus Productivity

The cost factors just outlined should continue to be recorded and analyzed for each new employee until his learning level is judged to be

---

[1] As of this writing, in 1973 the ceiling will be $10,800 and the tax rate 5.85 percent (paid by employee and employer).
[2] The taxable wage base will remain $4,200. The only exceptions to the $4,200 are Washington and Minnesota, where the taxable wage base is $4,800. Thus the $4,200 is the same base rate for federal and state; the difference is in the rate paid in each state. Federal and state unemployment insurance are two different tax bills (based on the same $4,200 ceiling, which is the first $4,200 of annual earnings). The ceiling is the same, but the rate varies by state.

at the average for his type of work and grade. Following this date there will be a period—the duration depends upon the aggregate amount of turnover costs for his job—when the company will continue to sustain production losses. These losses will cease when the employee's productivity reaches the breakeven point.

Learning curve analysis indicates that knowledge of the job must be coupled with experience before the employee can attain the breakeven point, and this takes time. This is *not* the point at which his productivity level equals his salary. The breakeven point occurs when his productivity offsets his pay to date *plus* all other costs incurred from the time of hire. Too many costing systems record breakeven points too early.

The True Cost of Labor Turnover

Labor turnover is defined as the total number of separations that occur during a specific period. Many of these separations are beyond the control of managers. Some separations can be planned in advance, such as retirements and economic slowdowns. The largest producer of separations is the employee who quits. He leaves without warning and sets into motion a chain of events that cost industry a great deal of money each year. The objective of this section is to provide the reader with both a theoretical analysis of cost incurred by separations and a method by which he can analyze his own cost of labor turnover.

Most accounting systems are not presently designed to provide managers with cost data on separations. In most cases executives must compile estimates of the costs involved.

The first cost category is incurred between the period of separation and replacement. For example, a ten-man work team is reduced to nine by a separation. Normally, either one of two occurrences will result. Productivity will drop because of the loss of the man's efforts, or an overtime schedule will be necessary to maintain productivity. In either instance, a real cost is incurred: the cost of productivity not achieved or the cost of overtime. These two criteria can be represented this way: Incremental profit per item multiplied by the number of items produced with one employee missing, or overtime rate multiplied by overtime hours required to maintain productivity at the normal level.

The second cost category involves recruiting and selection. This step is essential for replacement; yet its costs must be carefully analyzed. The activities of an established personnel or employment department should not be included unless separations are so numerous that overtime is required by the personnel department to process replacements. Normally, the activities of such departments have already been included in corporate overhead. A separate cost does exist in this category, which is not generally included, and is derived from the time expended by members of management in interviewing applicants for the position. If the vacancy had not been created by the man's quitting, the time consumed in interviewing would have been available for normal operational efforts. Assuming that today's executive is fully employed, it is logical to reason that the process of recruiting has reduced his productive efforts on the job.

Although no accounting records will record a cost expenditure, it does occur. Cost for this category is estimated by multiplying the department head's salary by the number of hours required to recruit and select one replacement. When applicable also include the overtime rate (personnel department) multiplied by the number of overtime hours required to recruit and select one new employee.

Training is the third cost category. The costs involve the number of hours of employee time directed to training the new employee multiplied by the average hourly salaries of the trainers. When applicable, also include overtime rate (training department) multiplied by the number of overtime hours required to train one new employee.

The fourth cost category, which has received the most attention, involves the differential between the new employee's salary and his productivity. Salaries are fixed. Productivity is variable. Some important variables in productivity are knowledge of the job and experience. One approach that might be helpful is the application of Bayesian statistics to the problem. The information required is the average total salary paid during the period between hiring and the breakeven point, and the average total contribution of an employee who leaves prior to the breakeven point and the percentage of employees who quit before the breakeven point is reached. This information can be used to develop the following model:

> Average total salary paid to an employee who quits prior to reaching the breakeven point minus the average total contribution made per employee who quits prior to reaching the breakeven point multiplied by the percentage of employees who leave before the firm reaches its breakeven point.

This formula can be demonstrated by a model developed by Thomas Zimmerer: "On the average, 5 percent of our employees quit prior to the firm's breakeven point being reached. Their average salary was $700 per month. We employ approximately 100 new employees per year and those who quit prior to our seven-month breakeven point stayed six months. Their contribution during the six months was approximately $3,000." [3]

$$\$700/\text{mo.} \times 6 \text{ mos.} = \$4,200$$
$$\$4,200 - \$3,000 = \$1,200$$
$$100 \text{ employees} \times 5\% = 5 \text{ employees}$$
$$\$1,200 \times 5 = \$6,000 \text{ per year}$$

Intangible Cost Factors

Intangible costs arise from many sources: the depressing effect that turnover has on morale, accidents and absenteeism as functions of low morale, reduced management efficiency and effectiveness, missed production schedules, the breaking of well-knit work teams, increased overtime, overhiring in an effort to maintain work schedules, the lower productivity of temporary employees.

The breaking of work teams has a double impact on productivity. One is obvious: When a worker leaves a five-member team, 20 percent of the production capacity is lost, forcing one or more of the five members or substitutes to work overtime to maintain normal productivity. But production capacity may still not be sufficient to offset the 20 percent loss. Moreover a premium is being paid for overtime, which will increase the standard cost per unit produced; thus a shipping date will be met, but the profit margin will dwindle.

The other effect of turnover on a work team is less obvious but can translate into significant intangible costs. A team is a collection of people—whether professionals, engineers, technicians, or clerical personnel—who have learned to work effectively together. Over time they have developed common interests, goals, and values. Each worker knows what he can expect from the others in terms of individual and group productivity. A team spirit forms as a result of compatible and mutually supported interpersonal relations. The unification of the group is intensified by external pressures, shared achievements and failures, the identity of each member with the group, and pride of membership. The group evolves as a self-protecting and self-perpetuating mechanism.

Thus when turnover strikes a team, it is reasonable to expect some percentage of production loss due to team breaking. Turnover costs as a result of team breaking can be substantial. And it might be noted that such teams probably offer the most effective form of turnover control.

[3] *Management of Personnel Quarterly,* University of Michigan, Summer, 1971, p. 11.

Capturing Management's Attention

Statistics that only enrich a company's archives are worthless. The purpose of turnover cost analysis is to capture management's attention. Detailed studies do not reduce turnover. What reduces turnover is positive corrective action. Turnover is behavior; it is attitudes and feelings turned into action. Turnover statistics serve no other purpose than to stimulate management to explore the causes of that behavior with the aim of solving one of its costliest problems.

Analytical turnover studies pinpoint problem periods as well as areas. Trends can be plotted weekly, monthly, quarterly, semiannually, and annually. All figures should be calculated for sections, departments, territories, and plant sites in terms of both numbers and dollar amounts. These exercises allow predictive studies to be made; for example, fluctuations in expansion and separation can be tracked during periods of high productivity and be used as the basis for projecting future turnover.

While no one can dispute the need for planning or the desirability of taking as many surprises out of the future as possible, using turnover studies for this purpose alone treats the symptoms, not the ailment. To meet its full responsibilities to shareholders and employees, management must move from description to diagnosis and cure. Calculating rates and costs of turnover attracts attention to the problem. Commitment to its solution requires an investigation of its causes.

SIX

pinpointing the causes of turnover

MANAGERS view rising turnover data with alarm. The more enlightened will realize that the problem cannot be wholly caused by bad employees who have infiltrated the organization. They were apparently good enough to be hired, and unless utterly lax employment practices were used, other reasons must prevail. The inclination to worry that something is wrong *somewhere* is a healthy one because it suggests investigating the roots of the problem.

The tendency is to fix on an isolated situation in the organization as causing turnover. If 20 people quit in a given month, it is seen as 20 different problems needing to be fixed. Theoretically this could involve 20 different and even conflicting solutions taking place in several functional areas of the organization. The result could be chaotic. Each case may of course have only personal reasons behind it. But many or all may be the result of organization pathologies to which employees reacted.

What is needed is problem analysis and a reasonable time of incubation and discovery before corrective action is taken. The results should be a composite view of organization problems. In our example of the 20 people who quit, common personal characteristics, known organization problems, reasons for termination, historical trends, and suspected environmental contributors should be singled out and correlations sought among them. The interrelationships among turnover incidents are thus defined and common characteristics discovered. Because the turnover analysis program calls for information and interpretations of data from both line and staff personnel, it enlists all departments in a cooperative effort to unearth the causes of turnover.

It is true that programs designed to explore turnover add to the cost of doing business. Thus their cost must be added to total company turnover expense. No study should be launched until the cost of the program is compared with the dollar loss from turnover. If the program budget represents too large a percentage of overall turnover costs, either the program design is faulty or the problem is so minor that a study of causes is unnecessary.

The structure of the program, which must conform with the needs and capabilities of the organization, is the subject of this chapter. Low turnover is the rare good fortune of few American businesses of any size today. For the many organizations beset by sizable turnover, analyzing its causes must take high priority.

Attacking the Turnover Problem

Companies faced with high turnover take various approaches to the problem. A common one is to view it as exclusively the responsibility of the personnel or industrial relations department to solve. But the monthly turnover statistics produced by personnel or industrial relations rarely find their way into the mainstream of important business data. The figures on turnover activity, when it is accounted for, are usually distributed to only a select group of executives and managers. The report may invite short-term concern or the stern admonishment, "Do something!" But it will accomplish little more.

Some companies have gone farther and placed a limit on the amount of turnover that will be tolerated from a foreman or supervisor. When turnover approaches or passes the acceptable limit one, two, or three months in a row, he is fired. This form of punishment attempts to demonstrate the important role of the manager in turnover. This is potentially a more effective approach than dumping the turnover problem into the lap of industrial relations and represents the beginning of an important awareness.

This action, however, is not supported by efforts to identify the true causes of turnover in the department. The real or imagined ineptitudes of the foreman who is fired are seized upon as the answer, and upper management satisfies itself that it is eliminating the problem by simply eliminating the foreman. In the final analysis business has found that it is easier to identify who caused the turnover than what. A who is more visible than a what and is of course highly vulnerable.

The obvious illogicity in this approach is that those who appraised the supervisor and approved his promotion to managerial status are not fired; those who failed to train and develop him to deal effectively with people are not fired. Nor are those who failed to uncover the basic causes of turnover and introduce their findings into the employment and management process, or those who recruited, screened, interviewed, and employed the workers who terminated. In addition the fired foreman is now another turnover statistic; the cost to replace him is probably higher than it was a year or more ago; and his fellow foremen are no better prepared to deal with turnover than they were. Nothing constructive has happened.

Some companies have attacked the problem with imagination and a sense of mission, convinced that the solution to the turnover problem is not to be found in simply firing lower-level managers. These companies are few. In addition there is too little exchange of research findings among companies when research is performed. What little appears of value in professional journals is often written by members of university teaching staffs or doctoral students remote from the business arena who rarely attract serious management attention.

A corporate program to study turnover causes and attack them through organization team efforts takes time and costs money. The results it produces are rarely spectacular and may not seem worth the expense regardless of their value. It is upper management's responsibility to stimulate the ongoing interest of all employees involved in the program by insuring that it is well designed and by lending it unflagging support.

Designing the Turnover Analysis Program

Programs to determine the causes of turnover must be carefully planned. Their findings will not be reliable if they attempt to do too much too quickly and have insufficient information systems and capabilities to carry them through. The most successful turnover analysis programs are those that gradually build up turnover data, allowing time for correlations to be spotted and causes to be brought to light. Crash programs fail to earn the commitment and involvement of management.

The turnover analysis program model must fit the practical needs of the organization. When it does not management support rapidly dwindles. The following guidelines relate company characteristics to the scope and sophistication of the program.

Size. The turnover analysis program need not be extensive in small to moderate-sized companies. Their hiring practices are more open to investigation because there is usually a central source of employment and recruitment and fewer supervisors interview and make employment decisions. Selection criteria are more standardized than in larger corporations. The variety of reasons people leave is smaller, resulting in less complex data with which to deal.

Geography. Access to data is easier in companies housed in one location than in those with offices and plants widely scattered.

Organization complexity. The size and scope of the program expand with organization complexity, and technology compounds the need for sophistication. Multidivision corporations providing a wide variety of services, products, and processes and functioning under complex organization charts can be difficult to deal with even when only head count or rate of turnover is being calculated. In companies in which each major division is an independent profit center that must pay its own way, division heads must be convinced that analyzing turnover is worth the cost and additional effort. In organizations structured with numerous reporting units employing very few people, it is sometimes advisable to group these.

Manpower support. Adequate personnel in close proximity insure against network breakdowns and time lags. They must be given training for the program work and must understand the importance of accurate data.

Volume of hires and terminations. The degree of program sophistication and the number of people involved in its administration must be proportionate to the volume of hiring and turnover.

Available systems. Data may be recorded and processed by computer, semiautomatically or manually. The program design must take into account what systems are available to the various reporting units. Some well-planned manual and semiautomated systems can function with a surprising degree of sophistication at low cost and are quickly and easily modified to meet changing needs. A complex, cumbersome system that is costly and difficult to run, maintain, and modify may not respond to shifts in need.

The design of the program must be flexible enough to accommodate the differing levels of management willingness to absorb and provide data. Some managers want to be involved in infinite detail; others do not. Some are academically oriented and value process as much as results. Some want "quick and dirty"—expedient—research to bring the problem into manageable range, but they do not want to spend the time necessary to provide the contribution the program needs from them. The interest of the manager looking for quick answers can often be aroused by turnover cost figures given to him in repeated doses and special encouragement from both program personnel and his superiors.

When the design of the program has been established, research into the causes of turnover can begin. Much information surfaces when the deceptively simple question of who leaves is examined.

Who Leaves?

The question of who leaves the company can often be answered by readily available information. Most companies have a payroll advice procedure for removing terminated employees from pay status. The form typically contains the following basic information:

1. Name
2. Birth date
3. Sex
4. Department
5. Job title
6. Pay grade, pay code, or classification
7. Current salary
8. Date of hire
9. Date of termination
10. Reason for leaving

These items alone will provide enough information to inaugurate a substantial turnover analysis program. Only when these data have been dealt with effectively should additional sophistication be attempted. They give the program a starting point that is reasonable in terms of the amount of turnover, the budgeted costs for the program, what is known or assumed about turnover causes, and the target dates established for program results.

Age and Sex

Age, sex, and length of service frequently correlate with reasons for terminating. One company found by using these correlates that the average age of employees in some units was remarkably static. For example, employees in one department ranged in age from 18 to 25 years of age. When people over 40 were brought in, this created interpersonal problems, and the older workers became unhappy and quit. The same may be true of course in departments where the average age is higher. These hiring and selection patterns not only affect turnover but also represent poor retirement planning.

Data about the sex of terminees might be analyzed next. The number of male and female workers in each department and the whole company must be known. Companies may have units composed of only one sex; turnover analysis of these produces little statistically that can be applied companywide. Departments with a male-female mix may provide turnover data that will reflect the company's hiring practices.

Male-female turnover studies are productive when correlated with job grade or classification to show trends. Companies want to know whether men or women make more stable employees. This is partly a matter of curiosity in the traditional battle of the sexes. But it may become an important issue in helping a company develop equitable employment and compensation practices where women are concerned. A firm that finds it has few women employees in supervision or management positions for instance should examine its hiring and promotion policies closely.

United States Department of Labor statistics indicate that absenteeism and turnover rates are about the same for men and women. However, more men than women quit to relocate geographically, and a woman 45 years of age or older is more likely to terminate employment than a man of the same age.

Education background has an effect on turnover rate. Unskilled male workers show a higher turnover rate than unskilled women in the first three months of employment. Among college graduates in the age range 27–31, men are more likely to change jobs than women.

Job Classification and Pay Grade

Analyzing turnover by job classification or by pay grade or code isolates the categories of people leaving and usually provides more reliable leads than does analyzing by job title, which does not always accurately reflect needed skills or function.

The number of employees who leave a pay grade or job classification each month shows the points at which production processes are being hit by turnover. If this pattern continues it becomes possible to predict the effects upon production efficiency. Supervisors can then take the necessary precautions to avoid bottlenecks and begin analyses to help determine causes of the turnover. The employment function can be requested to recruit more strenuously for some jobs than others and to maintain a larger active file on these job categories until the problem is brought under control. Awareness of the pattern also makes better utilization of overtime and training activities possible.

Dates and Length of Service

The dates of hire and termination provide other insights and should be monitored. Companies finding a high correlation between turnover and month of termination should be able to spot causes readily: beginning of a school year, exceptionally hot weather, harvest time. If such a correlation proves steady over a certain period, it allows a company to predict high turnover months and to plan ahead for the necessary replacements.

The average length of service of those leaving can be calculated in months from the hire and termination dates. When this is done for each pay grade within departments, it is possible for a company to determine how long after employment people leave and at what stages of training and productivity. The cost ramifications are significant. Short-service terminations prevent the company from recovering employment, training, and production loss costs. Long-service terminations represent losses in invaluable experience, well-developed skills, and work-team efficiency, and they can affect morale deeply.

Why Do They Leave?

In the early stages of program development, it is best to restrict the study to six major categories of reasons for termination: voluntary, involuntary (discharges), reduction in the work force, leave of absence (if counted as turnover), retirement, and death. This is done for each pay grade within each department. However, stopping here may obscure important if sometimes subtle facts necessary to guide the turnover reduction program accurately. Causes of turnover can be classified in more detail as follows:

1. Pay practices.
2. Causes directly associated with the job, such as poor working conditions, long hours, excessive travel, dislike of the work, and too much pressure.
3. Causes associated with supervision, such as unfair practices, inept leadership, lack of qualification, and abrasive personality.
4. Lack of promotion opportunities and chances for advancement, with typical complaints including lack of recognition and curtailed authority and responsibility.
5. Personnel policy and practices and work rules.
6. Interpersonal conflicts with fellow employees.
7. Personal reasons, such as return to school or home, need to care for children, relocation of husband, transportation or baby-sitting problems, change in career objectives, poor health, and death.
8. Involuntary causes, which include discharges, reductions in the work force, and forced retirement.

Some companies use checkoff lists to record causes. For example, one firm records only five basic categories, while another gives terminating employees sheets containing more than a hundred possible causes and asks them to check the appropriate ones.

Many companies include "Other employment" in the list. But this is not a *cause;* it is a *result* of causes within the employment situation. Using this entry one company found that 80 percent of its voluntary terminees gave it as their reason for leaving. This is hardly startling since the only other possible reasons would be poor health, death, voluntary retirement from the labor market completely, or leave of absence. Thus the employer expended a great deal of effort for nothing —he still did not know what caused the 80 percent to leave. He knew only that 20 percent were conceivably out of the labor market. This knowledge contributed little to his identifying and solving the company's turnover problem.

Correlations Reveal Turnover Causes

Correlations of two or more of the payroll advice data can give a strong indication of a turnover cause even if the employees in question do not stipulate their exact reasons. Some companies find for instance that more of their male than their female workers quit for a "better job." This vague locution perhaps expresses greater upward occupational mobility for men in the labor market coupled with more restrictive job opportunities for women.

By analyzing the dates of hire and termination, some companies employing large numbers of unskilled laborers have found that terminations coincide with the months when farmers pay a premium rate to workers to harvest the crops before the weather changes. One firm found that 40 percent of those hired in May and June who were between the ages of 18 and 26 left in September and October to return to school. In another company a large percentage of women left in early and mid-June; it took little research to determine that these were mothers who wanted to be with their children during summer vacation. Early spring and fall are times when many terminations of exempt employees take place.

A natural correlation is often found between length of service and reasons for terminating. Analysis may indicate that short service is due to poor screening and interviewing, inadequate orientation, improper job placement, ineffective training, a department practice of assigning the dirty work to newcomers, weak supervision, low morale, or interpersonal relations that make it difficult for a new hire to become a part of the in group. Long-service terminations are more difficult to analyze, but the four most prevalent reasons given for leaving are low pay, lack of development and advancement opportunities, low job satisfaction, and changes in the employee's personal life. Deaths occur in this group more frequently than in shorter-service groups. So do leaves of absence and retirements.

Examples of Analytic and Predictive Data

The following are a few examples of turnover analysis data from various companies, some of which the author developed. Note that some of the data have predictive qualities. Note too that some indicate clearly a company's concern about a particular group of employees or a specific reason for termination. The data were recorded and processed by computerized, semiautomated, and manual systems, and all the analyses provided management with various means of taking positive action to reduce turnover.

In Company A 58 percent of turnover attributed to personal or transportation reasons involved semiskilled female workers between the ages of 18 and 25 who were divorced and had children. Interestingly 60 percent of this group were from rural areas.

In Company B married male college graduates between the ages of 28 and 33 holding a master's degree had a higher turnover rate than those in the same age group holding only a bachelor's degree. Performance appraisals showed no significant differences between the two groups on the job, but the former were more marketable.

Sixty-one percent of the executive secretaries who quit the XYZ Corporation had college degrees, were either divorced or single (and when married had fewer children than women in any other occupation category in the company), and quit between the third and fifth year of employment to relocate. It was also found that they usually gave "personal reasons" for absences. The high ratio of college degrees reflected hiring practices.

At the PQR Company a solid trend indicated that management employees quit for reasons of job dissatisfaction within four months on the job or after 18 months of service but rarely in between.

Company C found that when the hiring rate accelerated in a given department, the turnover rate increased more than in any other department. But it also found that turnover increased in closely neighboring departments as well.

Company D found that turnover in some occupation categories decreased when IQ and other preemployment testing levels were lowered. This action helped prevent the hiring of overqualified personnel for routine jobs.

Company LMN experienced an increasing rate of turnover because workers were being fired for tardiness. Studies found that those fired actually lived *closer* to the plant site than most workers. The problem was thought to be linked to job dissatisfaction.

Company UVW found that high school dropouts were more likely to quit for health reasons than high school graduates and those with college background. Upon analyzing preemployment physical examinations, a team of physicians found no significant variation except that the college group was slightly heavier. The doctors recommended a more detailed preemployment physical and improved screening techniques, including psychological testing.

Alternate Research Methods

Companies often seek to pinpoint the causes of job dissatisfaction by going directly to the ultimate information sources—employees themselves. The exit interview, probably the best-established of these approaches, will be treated independently in the next chapter. Two other mediums of investigation are counseling and the attitude survey.

Counseling

There are similarities between counseling and interviewing. Both are communication processes requiring an exchange of ideas, leveling, and listening; both are concerned with the job satisfaction and productivity of the worker—his job history, strivings, needs, and problems; and both can have positive effects upon labor turnover.

One of the most significant differences is that employment interviewing leads to a specific end point, to hire or not to hire, whereas employment counseling typically has no predetermined objective except feelings of satisfaction. This is reasonable since the purpose of counseling is to diminish the worker's emotional problems. The employment interviewer's goal is not to alleviate the worker's distress but to amass the facts necessary to make a decision about employment.

Counseling provides the worker with an outlet for tension by encouraging him to sound off openly on questions that trouble him in either his personal or his job life. The complaints he may make about his work, company rules, or other employees show his reasons for discontent and may throw light on general causes of turnover. But the focus is on his feelings, not on how representative they are of significant organization problems.

The Attitude Survey

The purpose of the attitude survey on the other hand is primarily to uncover widespread causes of dissatisfaction before employee attitudes become so negative that termination is the only choice remaining. The attitude survey allows employees to gain recognition while on the job and a sense of proprietorship in the changes that result. It develops a participative and people-oriented work environment crosshatched with open channels of communication and feedback. Exit interviewing in the absence of attention to employee attitudes and needs appears to place more emphasis on the opinions of those who leave than on those of the workers who remain.

Attitude surveys can reveal subtle and often unsuspected causes of turnover. When responses are tracked over time, significant differences can be revealed between occupation groups in terms of personal needs on the job, the meaning of compensation, and career paths. One company for example discovered that its technical employees were more concerned about pay potential on their current jobs than about promotion opportunities and in fact had opted against promotion within the company almost to a man when offered it. They saw their jobs as training grounds, and they did not consider that the company was a place in which to invest years or that it treated its managers well. Another firm found that an overwhelming percentage of its sales and marketing people were intensely interested in promotion opportunities but that few channels for advancement were available to them because of management's misconception about their career objectives.

Ultimately a combination of approaches to the problem of turnover causes is probably best. Each company should tailor its methods to the scope of the turnover it is experiencing, the level of sophistication demanded by organization characteristics, and the human capabilities of the managers and employees who will be carrying the research forward.

Organization Responsiveness

The time lag between discovery and interpretation can cripple the best-planned program. This is true in research and development, market testing, and production technology. It can also be true in turnover analysis.

Turnover studies rarely produce fast-breaking definitive answers. No sweeping judgments should be made about personnel policies, work rules, compensation programs, vacation accrual systems, or disciplinary methods and other forms of administrative control until all available turnover data have been gathered and probed for correlations and indications of trends. These findings of themselves yield insights into the turnover problem, and they gain sophistication when they are analyzed by managers from all levels of the organization who have knowledge of the company's operations and can draw informed conclusions about turnover causes.

However, management can be sluggish or can procrastinate, slowing the program by failing to take timely action on the data. The turnover analysis program should anticipate this. Some ways to shorten these delays and stimulate attention are to strengthen predictive methods where possible to enhance the value of the findings, to establish followup systems requiring a written response from those receiving turnover reports, and to work turnover performance data, particularly financial figures, into the mainstream of management information as quickly as possible.

SEVEN

exit interviews: pros and cons

EXIT INTERVIEWING is one of the most controversial turnover analysis methods used in business. It is based upon the premise that if you want to know why people leave, ask them.

Companies differ widely in the uses they make of the exit interview itself and in their approaches to the information provided by the employee. Some of these practices are improper and contradict the purpose of the exit interview: to uncover the causes of turnover.

Some firms use terminal interviews merely to confirm established prejudgments about employees, policies, or supervisors under question. Many top executives are reluctant to institute the changes indicated as needed, although they may make minor concessions, because of multiple interpretations of the information they receive—the interviewer's, the employee's, and their own.

A company may refuse to admit that exiting employees are capable of bringing facts to the attention of management that the management team could not uncover. Sometimes the insights provided by the exiting worker are wholly ignored on the assumption that most employees exaggerate, some cover up bad situations to prevent a bad reference later on, some are disloyal or troublemaking, and some have an ax to grind and want to air their injuries, real or imagined. The exit interview in such cases is an institutionalized fraud preserved by the company because of employee pressures, competition from other businesses in the community, or a desire to give the impression of "listening."

Some companies feel that it is best to mollify terminating workers where possible for the sake of public relations. The interviewer may sympathize or agree with the employee even to the extent of pretending to take sides with him against the company in the hope of disarming him. The employee is unlikely to believe the charade, and the exit interview is a sham from that point forward.

Occasionally exit interviews are used as a means of trying to persuade employees to remain. The interviewer concentrates on clearing up misunderstandings and will make commitments or concessions. If these cannot be followed up, the employee will eventually leave. If the employee stays, moreover, he has been rewarded for his threats of quitting, and this may set a precedent the company wants to avoid.

Many firms on the other hand do utilize exit interviews validly. Some require transcriptions of interviews containing as much detail as possible. These are circulated with the request that the supervisors of the exiting employees comment on the statements contained in the transcripts. The personnel department is requested to conduct its own investigation, and all versions are then analyzed by top executives, who may conduct hearings or other investigations.

The Interviewer

Companies that use exit interviewing ordinarily assign responsibility for it to a representative of the personnel or industrial relations department. Rarely do supervisors conduct formal exit interviews. This is because the employee who is dissatisfied with the department's operation in general or the supervisor in particular is unlikely to discuss these matters with him for fear of antagonizing him and risking a bad reference in the future. In addition supervisors blamed by employees for various problems within a department are not likely to pass this information along to management.

Personnel on the contrary is a neutral place, a businesslike office where identification badges, cards, and other company properties kept by the individual during employment are turned in and where terminal checks are given. Personnel people also seem the logical choice for conducting exit interviews because of their familiarity with the interview process. The weakness in this argument is that while there are interviewing techniques fundamental to both exit and employment interviewing, the former can be more emotionally charged and require special handling.

All exit interviewers should be given special training in terminal interviewing and cataloging techniques and procedures. Even though individual differences may affect the outcome, training can help reduce extreme inconsistencies. The role of the interviewer should be a neutral one. He should not defend management or otherwise attempt to "educate" the employee. This defeats the purpose of the interview. "Education" has no practical use at this point because the employee is leaving and it will not benefit the organization.

It is helpful to assign the same interviewer to the same payroll classification of employees for a fairly lengthy period. If the same people interview hourly-rate production employees, for example, they become familiar with shop talk and existing problems, are better able to analyze the data presented to them, and can build subsequent questions that have perspective and significance. The assignment should be changed during the year (from hourly to exempt, say) to deepen interviewers' understanding of companywide problems and to prevent them from becoming so familiar with certain complaints through repetition that they lose objectivity and fail to analyze each problem situation on its own merits.

The Exiting Employee

Because exit interviewing must be voluntary and cannot be forced upon the employee, he has the right to refuse to give one. Most employees who have been discharged—and a company will sometimes seek interviews with those it has fired—do not want to participate. When they do they demonstrate considerable anger and emotional stress. Most voluntary terminees do agree to participate. Their reasons can vary. It is important for interviewers to analyze and make rapid judgments about the motives of each employee.

Some exiting workers use the occasion to attack a supervisor or vent pent-up dislikes and frustrations. When an employee who is invited to participate in an exit interview responds angrily, "You'd better believe I want to," he has been preparing for the occasion. He has probably reviewed a number of items to discuss and is eager for the opportunity. He is not concerned about the confidential nature of his remarks; he simply wants to be heard.

Many employees feel that the exit interview represents the only occasion on which management is recognizing them personally and is willing to take time to hear their views. Seeing the interviewer as a representative of management, they therefore feel that for a few minutes they have the ear of the top executives. Employees who might otherwise remain silent and avoid the exit interview are sometimes persuaded to participate because of the personal recognition it provides. In addition they may feel freer than during their employment to say what they want since they are now beyond the threat of punishment and the lure of reward.

Some employees are angered by this form of recognition. They insist that if management had taken the time to ask their opinions before they quit or had done something about the problems when reported by other terminees, it would not be necessary to hold an exit interview with them now. In spite—or because—of their bitterness, these employees want to participate in exit interviews; they need little coaxing. The problem for the interviewer will be putting their statements in proper perspective while maintaining reasonable control of the situation.

Employees who hesitate to participate are generally afraid that what they say may be used against them in the future when they need a reference or if they ever want to return. They may not trust the exit interviewer or the system because they know how the grapevine functions within the organization. They may have a sincere desire to help the company improve working conditions and are thus willing to review their reasons for leaving, but they do not want to attack anyone personally and fear their remarks may be construed as such.

These employees often feel a strong sense of guilt during the exit interview when they are called upon to discuss their supervisors or other individuals who played an important role in the decision to leave. Sometimes they will tell the exit interviewer only what they would say to their supervisors. They experience conflict between basic loyalty, which inhibits them from being openly critical, and a desire to comply with the request that they give an exit interview. Thus they see the exit interview as destructive rather than constructive, a threat to their values and their peace of mind.

These employees need and want reassurance that there will be no adverse consequences of any kind in connection with their remarks. An explanation of how the procedure works is helpful in establishing credibility with them and allaying their anxieties.

Forms of Exit Interrogation

There are many ways of requesting information from terminating employees. Some companies use interviews alone. Others ask the employee to complete a questionnaire. They often do not require the name of the employee if they do not intend to follow up with an interview.

Some questionnaires have a closed design. The employee is restricted to answering "Yes" or "No," checking applicable reasons for termination, or selecting among forced multiple choices. Others contain questions calling for essay answers.

Questionnaires requiring forced-choice, checkmarked, or yes–no responses have the advantage of leaving no leeway for variation, making them easy to tabulate. When they are sensitively correlated with the known personal characteristics of the exiting employee, they can produce data that are startling, bringing together new correlates and opening new avenues for action with a minimum expenditure of staff time and effort.

They have drawbacks, however. The impersonal approach does not allow for the elaboration possible during interviews, and results may be superficial and misleading. Predetermined reasons, unless very numerous, may be inapplicable to a significant percentage of employees, who either do not respond to questions or select answers that are not accurate for them but are only closest to being true. Moreover, predetermined choices developed after arduous research and systems development are not easily changed; thus they may be used long after some of the reasons have become irrelevant. Studies have shown that as many as 20 percent of some exit interview questions were never checked, yet continued to appear on questionnaires. They were simply recorded as "No" answers.

Questionnaires may be completed in the personnel office before the issuance of terminal checks and the return of identification badges and other formalities, or they may be mailed to former employees' homes.

The reasoning behind mailing them is that as several weeks have passed, the employee's emotions may have subsided sufficiently to allow him to develop a more "objective" view of his termination. Typically, however, only a small number are returned; 20 to 25 percent is often considered good. This weakens the sample and renders it inconclusive.

When the questionnaire is used as the starting point for an exit interview, several approaches can then be taken. One is simply to review the answers with the employee. The interviewer confirms that the employee has completed all items or verifies that he has interpreted the employee's remarks as they were intended. In the second case the intent is not to elicit more information, although it is usually given. The interviewer should ask to include these additional remarks in the questionnaire and not do so until permission is given. Another approach is to use the questionnaire as a springboard for further discussion.

The Exit Interview

The company sets the stage for exit interviewing by offering the employee the opportunity to participate voluntarily, assuring him of management's interest in his opinions, expressing concern about his leaving, requesting his help in improving the circumstances of employment, and indicating the punishment-free nature and the confidentiality of the interview.

The question of confidentiality must be handled honestly. In small companies with relatively low turnover rates or in small departments with stable employment, there is little chance of maintaining the anonymity of the exiting employee. Similarly, if a supervisor or manager leaves who is well known to upper levels of management, his quitting cannot go unnoticed. The interviewer loses credibility if he gives an employee excessive assurances of confidentiality when both know the realities of the situation.

The interview should be held in privacy, without people passing through the area or within hearing distance and without telephone interruptions. A closed door is conducive to openness in exit interviews because it is symbolic of confidentiality and seems to many employees to make the occasion more official and important.

Conducting the Interview

The interviewer must be sensitive to the emotional pitch of the employee during the meeting. This can often be detected by the tone of voice, facial expressions, and fidgeting and other signs of nervousness. Some women burst into tears before the interview begins, and some men vent their anger. In either case the interview should not proceed until the employee is reasonably calm or at least not exhibiting extremes of behavior.

Exit interviews should be kept short but must not be handled abruptly. The employee should be tactfully held to the subject but must be given enough time to express all key issues. The interview should be ended when the employee shows signs of fatigue or excessive nervous tension or when he has no more information to offer.

If the interview becomes lengthy because of the nature of the subject matter under discussion, the interviewer may want to take notes. There are two schools of thought about note taking. Some argue that it can distract the employee, causing him to pay more attention to the notes than the questions and to slow his delivery so that the interviewer will not miss anything. He may become upset if not all his remarks are noted or if items he considers only mildly important are recorded but not others that he feels are essential. On the other hand note taking may make the employee feel he is "down in writing" and thus cause him to become cautious. Writing the notes may also distract the interviewer, who may be so busy jotting down answers that he cannot sufficiently analyze what the employee is saying to pursue the point with a followup question.

Those in favor of note taking believe that it gives the employee tangible evidence of interest and concern. If action is to be taken subsequently, if a supervisor's reputation is at stake, or if major decisions need to be made following other exit interviews, accurate notes are needed because human memory is often unreliable.

The desirability of writing notes thus depends on how the interview is to be used and what effect note taking has on the employee. A general rule is that it is more important for the interviewer to understand the reasons the employee is leaving than to record his words. It would be unproductive to stop a free-flowing exchange to take notes.

Open-Question Techniques

Much of the interviewer's success in eliciting useful information is a function of his skill in questioning. Questions should be open-ended; that is, they should require more than a "Yes" or "No" answer. Limiting the employee with closed-ended questions prevents a free flow of communication.

It is usually best to give the employee an opportunity to become comfortable in the interview process before posing sensitive questions. He must be helped to gain self-confidence and trust in the interviewer. One way of building rapport is to make neutral yet germane inquiries—

for example, "How did you happen to join the company?" Other icebreakers might include questions regarding prior work experience. This information can be valuable. The interviewer might also ask the reasons for leaving other jobs and keep these in mind while conducting the interview. Special note should be made of similarities because this helps put the statements in perspective later when the interview is being evaluated.

Once the employee has had the opportunity to answer opening questions successfully, this will relax him and help the conversation flow. At this point specific and sensitive questions can be asked. The challenge facing the exit interviewer is to prevent the questions from sounding prying or threatening. For example, "How is it that you decided to leave?" is more effective than "Why did you quit?"

The first question implies that the employee has made a decision that the interviewer respects and accepts. It is aimed more at the process of decision making than at the decision itself. The second question is demanding and harsh and puts the employee on the defensive. It offers no way for him to defend himself. In the first question the employee can speak to the decision; in the second he must speak to his defense. The word *quit* in an exit interview moreover has a connotation that almost always makes it a value judgment. *To quit* is to give up, to surrender, and in our culture this is dishonorable. The words *leave* and *resign* are less accusatory and less value-laden.

When the interviewer wants a point elaborated, the way he asks for the elaboration will determine how much he gets. For example, "That's an interesting point. How did you arrive at that?" will elicit more information than "What did you mean by *that*?" or "Give me more detail" or "Why did you say that?" which are argumentative in wording and may stifle the employee. If the interviewer is skilled, he may need only to comment, "Now, that's an interesting point," and say no more. His vocal inflection and manner will invite more detail, and he often will get it.

Another technique that is effective in eliciting elaboration is silence. When the employee finishes his answer, the interviewer continues to look at him with an expression of anticipation. The implication is that he is waiting for more information. The employee, feeling uncomfortable because his answer seems to be inadequate or simply because he dislikes silence, takes up the question again and elaborates on his answer.

All questions asked should be directed toward situations and away from individuals. For example, if the subject of the supervisor arises, the interviewer should be aware of the tension he can create by asking the employee to speak about or against any fellow worker. Some terminees need little prodding, but others may require encouragement. In either case the interviewer can appeal to the knowledge and intelligence of the exiting employee by asking, "In your best judgment how might Mr. Harris function more effectively?" The question provides high levels of personal satisfaction and recognition and gives the employee the opportunity to exercise judgment. It is appealing to the ego. At the same time it does not discredit Mr. Harris. It communicates the basic assumption that a member of the company's management is doing well but that everyone can do even better. Asking the employee, "What's wrong with Mr. Harris?" or even just, "What did Mr. Harris do?" is accusatory and puts the employee in the position of attacking another person. This kind of question can make the exit interview unpleasant and generally unproductive.

Asking how the supervisor might function more effectively allows the employee either to give the reason for his dissatisfaction without reading off a list of accusations or to provide indirect clues to the problem. It makes the question more tolerable because of the unspoken understanding that not everything is wrong with Mr. Harris. It lets the employee answer, for example, "Mr. Harris could give everybody a little attention instead of giving a lot of attention to just a few people." The employee is not saying that Mr. Harris plays favorites and has his pets. But the implication is there, and that may be sufficient.

Analysis of Interview Data

Exit interview results can be highly misleading unless considerable caution is used in dealing with the data. The problem is twofold: interpreting the contents of each interview to determine the validity of the comments, and synthesizing the findings of all interviews to uncover the sources of trouble. Turnover analysts must weigh the motives and intentions of each employee and put his comments in reasonable perspective before they can judge which causes are subjective, which firmly indicate conditions requiring change, and which are borderline warranting further investigation.

Interpreting the Interview

One of the weaknesses of the exit interview procedure is validity. An obvious difficulty is that of determining the credibility of the employee. Some terminees use the interview for nothing short of character assassination. This is their moment to get even and to make sure that "so-and-so" is properly dealt with for having made their lives miserable.

Aware of this all-too-human inclination, some turnover analysts overcompensate by doubting the validity of almost any reason given for termination except a better-paying job or changes in the worker's personal life. Employees who quit complaining of doomsday jobs typically lack credibility. They may be considered troublemakers who would be leaving anyway. It may even be falsely assumed that those remaining do not find their jobs so dismal.

It is not uncommon for an exiting employee to bring into the interview the sentiments of others on the job who hope to make their complaints known to management but who are fearful that they will jeopardize their jobs if they "tell on the boss." This is particularly likely to happen when there are no reliable channels open to employees by which to share their feelings with management. Although this information should be noted and investigated independently, it should not figure in the evaluation of the exit interview data if it has nothing to do with why the terminating employee is leaving.

The task of interpretation is complicated when the employee does not give concrete reasons for leaving but indicates some vague, abstract causes that cannot be pinned down. The analyst should focus on reasons that are at a relatively low level of abstraction. The acceptable level of abstraction is not an arbitrary matter. The analyst must keep in mind that solutions cannot be applied to generalizations. If turnover is to be remedied, the specific causes must be defined. Note the following example of how abstraction can obscure an exiting employee's reasons for leaving:

ABSTRACTION LEVEL 5	"People aren't friendly."
ABSTRACTION LEVEL 4	"No one helps me."
ABSTRACTION LEVEL 3	"They don't answer my questions."
ABSTRACTION LEVEL 2	"They don't know the answers to most of my questions."
ABSTRACTION LEVEL 1	"The supervisor is never around, and there's nobody else in charge to answer my questions."

Possible assumption: Workers are insufficiently trained as evidenced by the fact that most cannot answer basic questions about a fellow worker's job. The supervisor does not spend enough time in the area; nor does he designate a representative when he will not be available.

The problem seems therefore not to be one of social maintenance, as might be thought were the remark at abstraction level 5 taken as the true cause, or of personal maladjustment, as the reason recorded at level 4 suggests. The turnover remedies must relate to the causes of the problem revealed at levels 2 and 1.

Synthesizing Interview Findings

All exit interviews should be analyzed in terms of basic issues and the findings synthesized to uncover the causes of turnover. Tabulation should be kept of primary causative elements in the work situation, miscellaneous problems that aggravate the primary causes, and so forth. These tabulations should be recorded for each job title, department, and division as well as for the company in total.

It is valuable to record under the heading "Frequency" the number of times since a given date that each reason for termination has been given. This not only provides a measurement but also helps identify where problems are occurring. The interview analysis should then classify turnover causes according to their origin: within a department (difficulties with a supervisor, specific work conditions, poor equipment) or in the company as an entity (pay policy, vacations, benefits, hours). There are also external reasons for termination, as Chapter 6 indicated. Female employees relocating because their husbands have been transferred are indeed leaving the company but for no reason associated with the job. The same applies to mothers and wives returning to the home and employees leaving to attend school. In each of these and similar cases, exit interviewing produces nothing of significance about job- or company-related circumstances causing turnover.

In assessments of internal causes of turnover, it is necessary to verify injustices or inconsistencies before action is taken, particularly if the action will discredit another employee (whether manager or subordinate). Too much emphasis is often put on too small a sample of exit interviews. It is always dangerous to jump to a conclusion on the basis of a single interview. It is even risky to accept the evidence of several interviews that occur about the same time because of the possibility of conspiracy. If the same issues are brought up for discussion by a number of terminees over time, this is a fairly reliable indication that a bad situation exists.

Occasionally exit interviews of management personnel receive heavier emphasis than those of other employees. While it is true that managers may have a broader picture of company operations and can be expected to lend greater perspective to their remarks, they may be as emotional in their responses as any other employee. Certainly any resigning manager who has held a trusted position in the organization and whose competence and motives are unquestioned may have valuable insights to share if he was unable to do so during employment.

On the other hand turnover analysts may give less or no weight to complaints made by terminees in low-graded jobs. This is especially likely if the employee has been discharged. Yet his version of why he was fired and what might have prevented it can be productive information. The company has an obligation to investigate his charges, at least to the extent of watching for repetition. If a supervisor continues to fire employees, the company may find that he is doing so without proper justification, without having taken proper steps to provide workers with counseling or training, or for the same few reasons all the time. In this case an immediate review should be made of the supervisor's qualifications and methods.

Advantages and Disadvantages of Exit Interviews

The advantages:

1. Immediate feedback on causes of terminations.
2. The opportunity to persuade employees to remain.
3. Data that can direct management to solving problems causing turnover.
4. A means of tracking management's progress by simply monitoring the frequency of reasons for termination.
5. A human touch that indicates the organization's interest in the individual.

The disadvantages:

1. Terminating employees may be emotional and thus distort their reasons for terminating.
2. Exit interviews are verbal and therefore difficult to qualitatively measure beyond broad topical categories.
3. The data may be affected by interviewers.
4. Many terminees do not confide in the interviewer because they are not convinced their remarks will be held in confidence and will not adversely affect a future reference.
5. Managers tend to distrust and thus discount statements made during exit interviews.

EIGHT

improving the employment process

ONE OF THE MOST effective ways to reduce turnover is to improve the employment process. The quality of the assessments at the entry point of manpower significantly determines the ability of the company to reach its objectives for years to come. Unless the selection system produces accurate predictions about the future performance of job candidates, it is a failure. Astute selection reduces the number of incidents in which people will need to be fired or will feel the need to terminate.

The object of the employment process is to get the right employee for the right job and to do so in the most economical way possible. While pay is of course an important factor in employment, workers want more than higher pay, a shorter work week, more vacation time, and improved hygiene factors. They want a feeling of contributing something worthwhile, even important, to the business, and this is made possible by better selection and placement methods.

Applicant Requirements

There are two fundamental qualifications that every applicant must possess. He must understand the nature of the work and be able to do it either immediately upon employment or after some reasonable amount of training; and he must be interested in the work and want to do it. For personnel specialists to do an effective job of recruitment, screening, and placement, they must determine that each candidate has these qualifications. This requires a thorough understanding of the economic and technological position of the organization and of the jobs that it needs to fill.

Company Needs and Job Requirements

It is obvious that a business on the brink of expansion or ready to make a significant breakthrough in a new area of technology needs a different kind of employee from one whose prospects are stable. Businesses that are expanding typically seek workers who are ready to move rapidly in their careers, able to make a significant contribution, and enjoy working in a fast track. Companies that are less dynamic in their growth, are maintaining the status quo, or are cutting back their operations may find it difficult to keep employees who want more than to hold to their present level of job skills, knowledge, and development.

Those involved in the employment process also need to be well informed on the requirements of each job opening in the company. They must know what education background is necessary, what previous related experience is required, how much initiative and judgment are called for routinely on the job, what physical demands are made upon the worker, and what mental or emotional strains the job may entail. In terms of responsibility, employment people must be apprised of the equipment or processes the employee will be dealing with, the kinds of materials used, the safety hazards, and the interdependence with other functions. Finally it is well for the employment specialist to understand the nature of the general working conditions surrounding the job.

Job descriptions should be made available to all employment personnel so that they will be better able to describe the position to applicants and to analyze abilities and interest more effectively.

Selection and Motivation

The selection process presents to a company an excellent opportunity to strengthen its motivation efforts as well as to bring into the organization people who can contribute significantly to the achievement of its objectives now and in the future.

Each person employed is asked to devote himself to the accomplishment of his job and to dedicate his energies, know-how, and aptitudes to the work at hand. The company for its part must be concerned with development and advancement opportunities, compensation programs, communication, and other activities that will support the efforts of the individual. This responsibility is easier to carry out when the employee enjoys his work, finds challenge in it, and gains recognition from it. It is much more difficult to execute when he is bored, degraded, or unchallenged by the job or simply does not like the work. The worker who does what he needs to do but no more is one who takes very little personal pride and satisfaction in his duties. That worker is the potential turnover case.

Every time a selection decision is made, it carries with it a prediction about how well the individual will perform on the job. Many times the selection process is so completely absorbed in determining whether or not an applicant can do the work that very little time is spent trying to determine whether he will want to. It is assumed that he brings with him enough personal motivation to want to accomplish the job. It is an important function of selection and placement personnel to verify that the candidate is predisposed to like the work and brings with him a degree of motivation that, once he is on the job, will stimulate him to high performance.

Recruitment Methods

Good recruitment methods pay dividends, but they do not develop by accident. It is important for those with employment responsibilities to conduct research to determine the best sources of referrals in terms of both number and quality of applicants.

The matter of availability of candidates is an important aspect of recruitment and can become crucial when the labor market is tight. No matter how skillful the selection and placement specialists may be, their hands are tied if so few candidates are available that they must judge applicants' abilities against minimum job standards. As the number of candidates increases, the employment people are able to evaluate them according to increasingly specific employment criteria. They first list all candidates who meet the minimum stated requirements of the job. From these names they select those who exceed the minimum requirements in terms of job skills, experience, and personality qualities deemed desirable. These applicants are listed in the intermediate category. From among these names are selected those who meet the unwritten, intangible demands or desires of executive and hiring managers above and beyond the intermediate job qualifications. These then become the serious candidates for consideration.

External Sources of Applicants

Employment agencies, executive search firms, school and college placement offices, minority recruitment sources, government placement bureaus, and periodical publications of various sorts are all able to call applicants' attention to job openings. There are times when certain local newspaper advertisements are better for recruitment than any other source. However, the company's employment office should maintain records on which sources have produced the best results for particular jobs it has needed to fill.

Much too often employment departments fail to keep records of the return of their recruitment investment. They continue to run ads in newspapers, professional magazines, and journals or to use other habitual channels without taking the time to analyze the effectiveness of their efforts. For example, one company located in a suburb of a large metropolitan center typically ran want ads in five suburban and two urban newspapers. A study of the pull of these ads revealed that nearly 40 percent of all applicants responded to only one of the seven newspapers and that three papers failed to produce enough applicants to warrant continued use of their help-wanted columns.

For the most part companies find that an ongoing program of recruitment is far superior to a one-shot effort. This applies to first-job or untrained personnel as well as to experienced production, clerical, professional, and managerial employees. The company must maintain contacts with sources most likely to produce qualified candidates.

Employee Referrals

One of the best referral sources continues to be current employees. A number of studies have shown that the most productive workers and those with the best attitude toward the company and their jobs are typically those who recommend it as a place of employment to friends. Not wishing to risk a good reputation with the organization, they typically refer applicants in whom they have confidence. Many companies find that these personal referrals produce new workers who have one of the lowest turnover rates of any category of employees and who become some of the best performers on the job.

The picture can be quite different if the candidate referred by a current employee is a relative. This is a problem shared by companies of all sizes, though very large firms with geographically scattered divisions or plants may not be confronted with it so often or acutely as a smaller concern in one location.

While the same selection criteria should prevail regardless of any connection a candidate may have with a member of the workforce, there is sometimes a tendency to hire a relative of an employee even though he may not meet all prescreening employment standards. In addition most companies that have had experience with hiring relatives find that when one is dissatisfied there is a good possibility of losing all.

Related employees seem to find it especially difficult to keep personalities out of the work situation. One company for example employed a husband-and-wife team, the husband in the computer division and the wife in an important processing job in the accounting department. After the firm decided to computerize its accounting records, the project seemed to bog down and became extremely costly. It was obvious that husband and wife were not able to cooperate though they had worked with one another indirectly for some time. None of the other employees was willing to complain about the inability of one spouse's department to meet the other's needs effectively, but they became disgruntled with the situation and a morale problem developed. Thus when relatives are hired, it is usually in the company's interest to assign them to unrelated departments.

Interviewing

The employment interview is the most sensitive function of the selection and placement process. After recruitment efforts have been completed, employment applications have been filled out and analyzed, and sometimes credit and work references have been verified, interviewing takes place. Interviewing may be used to identify qualified people for future reference or to screen candidates for a current opening. In either case it must be more than a tired and routine exchange.

Employment interviewing is an open communication process that elicits, clarifies, organizes, or synthesizes the information both participants need in order to judge the appropriateness of the applicant for a specific job.[1] Interviewing is also a social relationship because there is structured interaction between the two people, but it is fundamentally a sending and receiving process. The interviewer must be congenial and polite as well as subtle, but he must pursue the specific objective of obtaining usable information upon which to base a decision about the applicant. This must be his unyielding purpose.

When conducting a number of interviews for a given position, employment specialists can fall prey to the assumption that all applicants for the job are fundamentally the same. This is a fallacy that has caused companies to experience high turnover. Every candidate for employment is different from every other in essential ways simply because each is a human being. Only when these fundamental differences are recognized and efforts made to understand them will the search for predicters of success on the job be possible.

Round Robins

Some companies go to great pains to develop systems of multiple or round robin interviewing. A number of executives or managers interview an applicant, the objective being to learn as much about him as possible. The notion—correct in itself—is that knowledge of applicants reduces the margin for error.

Round robin theory demands, however, that all or a majority of those who interview the applicant come to the same or similar conclusions about him. They must at least see in him similar elements of potential success or failure. The value of each interviewer in the round robin is based upon how closely his opinion of the candidate conforms with that of other interviewers.

One weakness of this approach is that it tends to emphasize quantity over quality of investigation. There is reason to doubt that significantly more can be learned about an applicant in several days than might have been learned in a relatively short time by a single skilled interviewer. Another is that once the applicant is hired, there is often a misconception that all the company ever needs to know about him is already known. His performance as an employee is judged more by whether it

---

[1] See D. B. Peskin, *Human Behavior and Employment Interviewing* (AMA, 1971), p. 12.

confirms preemployment expectations of him than on its own merits. The original evaluations are retained years after hiring and are referred to when promotion opportunities arise. This practice can lead the performance appraiser to undervalue very real accomplishments because they do not correspond with the predictions made by the hiring interviewers.

Testing

One of the most controversial methods of employment selection is that of testing. Sometimes screening includes hours of job skills and general knowledge testing. Some companies retain consultants for the purpose of personality or aptitude assessment; tests that purport to measure these qualities are used because of the credence they seem to add to the selection process, but for the most part they have not succeeded in adding to the predictive quality of the selection process. Testing has been criticized as well because its use has often been arbitrary. The Civil Rights Act of 1964 and subsequent equal employment opportunity guidelines have brought testing under greater scrutiny.

The primary caution is that tests should be considered only in relation to a standard. Unless a test can be validated and its ability to predict success or failure proved, it is nothing more than window dressing. Rarely do companies conduct sufficient research to determine whether performance on the job was predicted by the test or whether in fact hiring decisions would be quite accurate without any tests being given. The best criterion for using tests must be whether or not they add accuracy to performance predictions. If they cannot help the organization make better decisions about applicants, they should not be used.

It is important to make certain that tests are used for the purposes for which they were developed and with an understanding of their limitations. For example, achievement tests rarely help determine a person's aptitudes. Personality tests, as already noted, may add nothing to the ability of the employment office to predict performance on a job unless a great deal is known about the work and the work milieu. General knowledge tests may or may not confirm that an individual has achieved a specific level of education.

The tests must of course be selected to measure what they are supposed to measure. There are two fundamental purposes of tests. They may be predictive tests, indicating whether the test taker will be capable of certain behavior in the future; or they may be achievement tests, confirming that the test taker can do certain tasks now. Employment specialists need to familiarize themselves with the tests currently available in order to choose which will serve their needs appropriately.

Intelligence Tests

One of the problems with general intelligence tests is to determine whether they measure mental power as it will be needed on the job. The classic definitions of intelligence—the capacity to adapt to one's environment and to environmental change or the capacity for abstract thought—may not be pertinent to the organization's milieu. It is not uncommon to find interviewers and placement specialists confusing intelligence measurements with general knowledge or even job skills tests. Many also do not understand the test specifications or the distribution of scores.

There is hardly a manager alive who does not want to fill a job vacancy in his department with an "intelligent" person. He may not be able to explain fully what he means by this. Some managers believe that the intelligent person is one who follows orders to the letter. Intelligence to some managers may mean the ability to solve complex mathematical problems or perform well on logic tests. Yet sometimes turnover is reduced in routine jobs if people with average or below-average intelligence are hired.

Verbal Skill Tests

Evaluating verbal skill epitomizes many of the problems faced by employment specialists in interpreting test results. Tests of verbal skill vary widely. Some include a list of several hundred words to be defined. Some require word usage. What these reveal about applicants is not verbal skill but vocabulary; they show simply that he is familiar with many words. This skill is rarely if ever significant in employment performance.

What is usually meant by *verbal skills* is the ability to communicate effectively upward, downward, and horizontally. Better managers communicate in simple, direct ways. The size of a vocabulary tells nothing about how it may be used. A large vocabulary can hamper downward communication because subordinates may be unable to respond to words and concepts they do not fully understand. Peers and superiors may consider the use of big words and complex sentences pretentious and unnecessary.

In many respects verbal skill in general vocabulary and communication ability are a function of leadership style and management philosophy. One way of evaluating these elements is to ask a management applicant to indicate how he would communicate a list of directives to employees. Given pertinent facts about the education and occupation of the subordinates, he will then demonstrate not only verbal skill but degree of people orientation and display a wide variety of clues about himself.

Vocational Proficiency Tests

A vocational proficiency test may confuse rather than clarify the picture of an applicant's qualifications by indicating a low profile while references indicate that he is particularly well suited for the work. Such contradictions can present a dilemma if the test has a long history of unquestioned use in the company. Doubt may be cast upon the employment specialist or the references.

It may well be that the test, the employment specialist, and the reference writers use different criteria and are not measuring the same quality. For example an employee may not have met all deadlines or production quotas but tried very hard and was considered a "good employee" by company A. To company B a "good employee" may mean one who meets quotas and deadlines. To it the reference is worthless, and it may reject the applicant because of the confusion. Company C may place equal emphasis on trying hard and meeting quotas, while company D places more emphasis on employee interest and willingness, confident that it can motivate an employee to high productivity if he shows a desire to reach achievement levels on the job. Thus vocational proficiency and job skill tests are effective only if they measure factors contributing to overall productive effectiveness or characteristics valued in the present workforce.

Some companies present applicants with situation questions in the form of case studies. The applicant is asked how he would solve the specific problem. While this kind of test is administered mainly to management candidates, it can produce excellent results in determining the skill level of assemblers, production workers, and clerical personnel. One company asked assemblers to indicate what they would do if a certain piece of equipment failed. The applicants who had the kind of experience the company desired were familiar with the equipment and could easily describe what their behavior would be in such a situation.

Testing the Test Taker

Many times a test score will reflect the ability of an applicant to deal with tests rather than predict his future behavior on the job.

Unfortunately some employment offices do not take this into account and give greater weight to test results than to the judgment of interviewers. A few percentage points on a test will lead them to select an applicant who may not be nearly so qualified as one who simply does not take tests well.

Most applicants have been tested and retested during their careers. They have seen many variations on a testing theme. In addition many management applicants, having been in management and read the classics, form an image of the kind of candidate most companies *will not reject*. They know how to avoid appearing to be a misfit.

Subjective tests give some applicants the opportunity to respond in a contrived way that masks their true feelings. Skilled test takers have learned not to reveal pessimism, lurking fears, or psychological problems. During interviews they rarely respond in the "wrong" way. To the overused question, "What is your major weakness?" they are likely to respond, "I'm impatient to reach objectives. Once I get a project rolling, I tend to drive pretty hard to finish it. I guess I push my people too hard some of the time, and that isn't always good." Thus the applicant reveals the safe weakness; who would reject a candidate whose major weakness is hard work and dedication?

Evaluating Test Results Against the Norm

Because the purpose of employment is not only to fill a vacancy but to upgrade the current workforce, the norm of the current employee group may be used as the minimum standard. Acceptable applicants will then be those who exceed the norm.

There are dangers if applicants exceed the norm by a wide margin. Candidates hired for supervisory and management positions who far exceed the intelligence level of those they work with are less effective because of a lack of sympathy for and understanding of those less "intelligent." They also sometimes assume superior understanding among those who report to them so that they fail to take a developmental approach to employees. Production workers whose skill level is above the norm may become bored and restless because their capabilities are greater than job demands.

The selection system must be sensitive to both applicant and organization and respond to them. Most tests are not refined enough to highlight the subtle factors that indicate overqualification. Employment criteria must therefore be drawn from more than test scores, which often make only gross distinctions about how much more or less an employee may be expected to do on the basis of experience and education and the minimum requirements of the job.

Measuring Intangible Qualifications

Certain applicant characteristics are virtually impossible to measure with standardized tests and must be assessed individually by an employment specialist, usually the interviewer. These evaluations require great powers of discernment on the specialist's part.

An interviewer will often look at the company's official list of characteristics that must be evaluated and make judgments in tandem. If he checks *motivation* in the favorable column, he has a tendency to indicate also that the applicant has a favorable *attitude*. He feels obligated to evaluate such concepts as *initiative* and *growth potential* in the same way. Interviewers tend to link ratings because they cannot discriminate between them conceptually and because the selection process may be insensitive to subtle distinctions. Moreover the effort may be fundamentally futile because, like the performance appraisal guidelines that often list these same kinds of attributes, the employment system may not actually give them significant weight in the hiring decision. Two qualities that companies usually do value and attempt to assess, however, are maturity and judgment.

Maturity and Judgment

One of the commonest pitfalls in predicting applicant effectiveness is the measurement of maturity. Applicants who are perceived as mature are often forgiven poor test results and even marginal references.

Maturity may hold an almost sacred place among a company's criteria for employment. Interviewers look for signs of it everywhere. It is easier for most interviewers to develop concepts (not always valid) about what immaturity is and work backward, assuming that the opposite of the signs of immaturity will represent maturity. Many confuse eagerness with immaturity. They will then judge the mature applicant as one who "does not come on like Gangbusters," avoids appearing to be aggressive, and seems to take matters in his stride. His aspiration levels may in fact be low, and he may be a nonachiever or a failure avoider who is not at all mature.

Evaluating intangible attributes of course requires that the interviewer rely on his perceptions. But he must keep in mind that his conclusions are subject to bias and must attempt to validate them against other capacities or skills demonstrated by the applicant. One of these is the faculty of judgment.

Judgment is often thought of as a key to maturity though it too is a difficult concept to define and evaluate. Certainly tests designed to examine verbal, problem-solving, and decision-making abilities help the interviewer reach reasonable conclusions about an applicant's judgment. When combined with interviewing techniques that are capable of providing insight about the applicant, the tests can be supportive.

Often the interviewer will ask the applicant to comment upon prior achievement or nonachievement in his career. Or he may question him on the future of a certain branch of technology or method with which the applicant is familiar. The purpose is more than to bring factual knowledge to the surface. Skilled interviewers want to observe the applicant in the process of analysis and judgment making.

Applicants for managerial positions who have skills and experience must be evaluated in terms of their ability to transfer their sense of judgment to a new situation. The interviewer must also evaluate in what ways the applicant's former jobs are similar to or different from the current vacant position. Applicants entering the management profession for the very first time must be evaluated for skills probably gained in school and for growth potential. Approaches considered helpful in evaluating the judgment of experienced managers may be useless when applied to newcomers to the field.

Elements of the Employment

The primary responsibility of interviewers and managers is to make a decision about an applicant. The decision is the outcome of solving the problem of whether to hire a candidate. The processes of problem solving and decision making are not fully enough understood by interviewers and managers to guide them in these exercises.

The Process of Problem Solving

The first step in problem solving is simply to define the obstacles that must be circumvented. When people problem-solve, they bring past experiences to bear on a present objective and attempt to apply relevant information. The objective in the employment process is to select an applicant to fill a job vacancy who not only possesses adequate skills, knowledge, and experience for the job now and in the future but will be found acceptable to the hiring manager.

At the beginning of the selection process, there are many alternatives because not so much is known about applicants as will be known later. Decision making is a process of selecting among alternatives those that seem to possess the greatest advantages and the fewest adverse effects. As more information is known about each applicant, the alternatives will become fewer and fewer. The final decision is a selection from among the very best alternatives.

In solving the problem of which candidates to recommend to the hiring manager, the interviewer or placement analyst must do three things: (1) relate each applicant's education and occupation background to the job description of the vacancy, (2) second-guess the hiring decision maker so as to send him the applicants most likely to be found acceptable and (3) predict the outcome of employing the applicants by comparing what he knows about them with what he knows about the circumstances or work milieu of the job.

When he analyzes the applicant's background, the interviewer attempts to correlate previous life experiences with job responsibilities. His initial interest is in experiences that contribute to the attainment of high performance on the job.

When the interviewer attempts to second-guess the hiring manager or supervisor, he may have to compromise his own feelings about each applicant. In his judgment the hiring manager may lack the fundamental skills needed to make personnel decisions. The interviewer may feel that the manager is simply not in a position to utilize the primary indicators of success or failure and will instead make his selection on the basis of personal impressions. In addition he may suspect that the manager will be pressured into basing his decision solely on the criterion of know-how because of the need to fill an important vacancy.

When the interviewer tries to predict the outcome of employing a given candidate, he is often handicapped by having insufficient facts on which to base his decision. In large organizations it is unlikely that the personnel specialist will have the opportunity to know whether his recommendation decisions have been correct. He knows when applicants for employment are rejected because he must then produce more applicants. But he may not be aware of the relationship between the factors used in the decision to hire and the factors that lead to the firing or resignation of the employee. A simple research model can be developed that compares the personal characteristics, education, and experience of those who resign or are fired, those who are considered to be acceptable for employment and hired, and those who are rejected for employment during a certain period.

Subjective Influences on Decision Making

Decisions are never wholly objective; they are always influenced, whether consciously or unconsciously, by values that the decision maker brings to the problem to be solved. Each observer of the perceptual field brings to every situation certain expectations and motives of his own. This is the stuff of which impressions are made.

The employment interviewer forms impressions about candidates from their physical characteristics, their gestures, and the manner and content of their speech. If he allows stereotypes to influence his judgment or lets the halo effect bias his opinion of them, he is hampered in his decision making. He has developed predispositions that lead him to read applicants' life experiences, attitudes, and even appearances and conversation styles, as evidence of success or failure. Decisions are distorted when the interviewer is conditioned by such beliefs.

What is happening of course is that the interviewer is being influenced by a set of circumstances or clues that he remembers were once either successful or unsuccessful in predicting the outcome of employment. The clues that the applicant gives will not be interpreted according to their actual value but will be given high or low dominance depending upon the interviewer's sensitivities.

The impact of mental set on the interviewer's evaluations may draw its strength not so much from the degree to which the applicant reinforces the interviewer's bias but rather from the number of times the interviewer runs hot and cold about him during the meeting. In either case mental set becomes a reference point in the employment process that causes the decision maker to reach invalid conclusions. The more aware the employment specialist is of his predispositions, the freer he will be to exercise his capabilities in making an effective selection decision.

How Selection Practices Err

Employment specialists have to face the fact that no matter how objective their selection criteria, no matter how alert they may be to potential distortions arising from their own values, the selection process is at best an uncertain guessing game. This is true regardless of the quality of the interview and the relevance of the tests given to applicants.

The interviewer can of course know whether or not an applicant can use a particular kind of equipment or has command of certain techniques that are minimally required on the job. But this is hardly decisive because the real test of employment decision making is not selection between typists and nontypists for a typing position, for example, but between typists and other typists. The selection system must be sensitive to more than simply the gross identifiable skills.

Experienced employment specialists know that no single selection philosophy applies in all or even a majority of cases. They have hired applicants who are believed to be well qualified and who have succeeded in fulfilling all expectations. These are of course not mistakes because what was predicted came to be. On the other hand, many interviewers have rejected an individual believed to be a poor fit or somehow unqualified. Is this a mistake? They can never know because the applicant who has not been hired cannot prove or disprove the hypothesis that rejected him. It cannot be assumed that the rejected applicant was the opposite of the one accepted. Usually the evidence is not that clear.

A typical employment decision may be to hire a marginal applicant simply because of labor scarcity and the pressure to fill a vacancy. The applicant may be successful and the interviewer is proved wrong. If the applicant eventually fails, the interviewer's judgment has again been proved wrong because he has hired the person who was only marginal to begin with.

Two Extremes

Some managers who must make hiring decisions will select in favor of an applicant they know the least about rather than take a chance on someone whose references and general qualifications are well known. After exhaustive reference checking, interviewing, and analysis, it is very likely that negative information about a candidate will be discovered. It may be that another applicant for employment cannot be so easily researched. If both have the same basic qualifications, managers are likely to take a chance on the least-known applicant rather than risk hiring one whose weaknesses they think they know something about. For this same reason it is not uncommon to find companies deciding against internal promotions and going to the outside to hire. They would prefer to avoid selecting people with known negative characteristics and find it safer to hire someone about whom they know considerably less.

Some companies believe, on the contrary, that by recruiting and hiring a person who exactly fits the qualifications for the job, has precisely the personality characteristics deemed acceptable by management, and has all the education and occupation background believed to be of value, the job will be perfectly filled and management need only sit back and watch the achievements flow. Such companies are often disappointed because few people can live up to that kind of expectation. The recruitment process is usually long and expensive, and the job lies vacant in the interim. And if the candidate who is eventually hired fails to meet all expectations, management assumes that the problem was simply a case of not having looked long or hard enough for the right person. This is analogous to the lost oarsman's being told to row harder. When another recruitment assignment arises later, it is conducted in the same manner and often with the same result.

The management of such a company is likely to take pride in its selection practices, believing that its standards of excellence are so high that today's crop of "would-be achievers" cannot satisfy it. Some companies go so far as to fire the "would-be achiever" rather than admit that their recruitment and selection strategy is erroneous. Undoubtedly it produces some excellent people, but when peers see this fine talent fired, the effect on their morale can be devastating.

The effect such a system has on the people hired is tragic. They find themselves facing continual defeat. The obvious truth is that no one will probably ever fully meet the expectations of the company, which will consequently view many of those it hires as compromise choices. As a result management may hesitate to enrich the employee's job, think twice before promoting him, and be highly sensitive to every misjudgment or normal faltering that he displays. The worker will have a great deal of difficulty living down the compromise image and as already noted may be fired because he has failed to live up to a myth through no fault of his own.

Long-Range Effects of Selection Errors

An applicant for employment cannot be considered a candidate until both he and the company's employment people see something of value in the relationship. Particularly in times of scarcity in the labor market, many applicants consult with a number of executive search firms and employment agencies and do considerable research in business and professional journals in order to get a line on companies in which they feel they will prosper both financially and professionally. They begin to form ideas about "good" and "bad" companies.

Word travels fast when a company is unable to keep highly qualified people, rejects good candidates because they do not have some minor qualification, or exercises arbitrary hiring practices. Its reputation in the job market can be critically damaged as a result, and it can come to be generally thought of as "unprogressive," "ultraconservative," or "resistant to new ideas."

While it is usually impossible to know the true nature of a company without having been employed in it, its hiring practices project an image of it that leads observers to make certain assumptions about it. These assumptions may not always be valid, but this does not prevent job seekers from acting upon them. A company whose image is unfavorable among a large proportion of available applicants for specific kinds of work has difficulty attracting enough candidates to make valid decisions about their capabilities. One of the best clues to this situation is the number of candidates a competitor interviews during the same period for comparable positions.

Upgrading the Selection System

Most organizations have faith in their selection systems though they would be hard put to justify it. While practically every other system in the organization is under constant scrutiny and is provided with objective measures of performance, the employment process remains immune, largely because of the mystique involved in human evaluation and selection. Selection techniques are assumed to measure factors that are related to job performance, but that is not always the case. It is only through valid research that fallacies and myths in the selection process can be corrected.

In addition most employment offices, recruiting within the narrow band of skills that the company can utilize, base their evaluations of applicants upon what are assumed to be the success criteria of the current work group. That is, the group's record of achievement becomes the standard by which applicants are judged. Employment specialists attempt to fill job vacancies by recruiting from the same sources and selecting from among people who have comparable background and experiences to those already employed. Thus the full capabilities of the company's selection system are difficult to measure because of the limited demands placed upon it.

There will probably never be a perfect employment process, but improving selection and placement methods will usually insure higher performance standards and a more stable workforce. These conditions make it possible for management to plan more effectively for its future needs. Selecting candidates whose potential seems good enables a company to develop its employees, give them cross-training, and generally broaden their capabilities so that new vacancies can be filled by transfers, reassignments, and promotions.

NINE

improving the promotion process

THE TIME IS PAST when a craftsman needed only his skill and his tools to go into business and grow with it. Today fewer small, new businesses survive, much less prosper, than ever before. Even within industrial organizations opportunities for spectacular advancement are few. The days of janitor to president are gone. Complex organization structures with internal demands for technological, managerial, and financial expertise inhibit the advancement of noncollege and nonprofessional people. For them climbing to the top is an almost impossible dream.

Even for professionals the climb is not easy. In many organizations there are few significant differences between many staff functions within divisions or departments. These jobs vary mostly in technique, making it relatively simple for the company to rotate people on jobs, effect lateral transfers, and enlarge (though not enrich) their jobs but reducing the opportunities for promotion. Multiple layers of management result in half-step advances that in some companies mean only modifications of titles.

Notwithstanding these limitations, which will be discussed in more detail later, the promotion process can be structured to provide satisfaction and motivation for workers and to enhance the stability and quality of the workforce as a whole.

An important aspect of a successful promotion program is that employees see it as equitable. This is a function partly of clear, well-formulated performance criteria and partly of open communication with employees regarding how the advancement system works and what checks and balances are included to prevent bias. Some companies give employees the opportunity to bid for available jobs, which not only involves them in the promotion process but heightens their competitive spirit. However, good judgment and enlightened administration must insure that competition is not allowed to create interpersonal conflict.

Job bidding requires feedback to employees who are rejected, a practice that should be incorporated into every form of promotion program. This serves as a means of confirming the objective nature of the system and reevaluating the criteria for promotion as well as providing an opportunity for counseling employees with regard to applicable strengths and needed improvements. It enables the company to express its interest in the career potential of its employees by discussing with them the challenges and obstacles arising in their jobs and exploring the experiences that support success, always relating these to the employees' backgrounds. Workers are not always willing to see flaws in their experience and should not be expected to agree with a decision not to promote them. But these discussions can serve as recognition of initiative and motivate continued improvement and development.

Performance Appraisal and Performance Criteria

Performance appraisal methods and criteria are important to a successful promotion system. Performance appraisal is the instrument by which the worker's accomplishments are measured. Production jobs are relatively easy to measure, as are other jobs on which the scope of the work is narrow, output can be counted, quality is apparent in a short time, and the skills, regardless of how many or how complex, are known.

Management positions are unlike these. The results of a manager's decision may not be known for months or even years. What is appraised is often not the outcome of the decision but the way the decision was made and the manner in which the recommendation was packaged, marketed, and eventually sold to upper management. One bad decision may not destroy the employee's chances for advancement because the failure may not be perceived until much later, and even then the decision cannot be wholly discredited if the causes of the failure are not known. A series of minor failures may or may not be disastrous even when they are closely linked. Thus the measurement of managerial performance is variable, often inconsistent, and affected by influences neither the appraiser nor the employee fully understands or can control.

Although some of these drawbacks are ineradicable concomitants of the complexity of modern businesses, others result from the failure of companies to define performance criteria. Organizations that do not develop appropriate criteria weaken the motivational impact of promotions.

Workers may become disgruntled and even quit if jobs into which they are promoted lack clearly defined objectives and functional relationships and if the promotees perceive that their superiors' expectations of them are confused. It is not enough to define a job on the basis of tasks and project assignments if the employee is required to piece together the important elements of the job as he would a jigsaw puzzle in order to discover its reasons for being.

When performance criteria are left vague, the door is opened to arbitrary judgments on an employee's effectiveness. The result can be a parade of workers in a job, all found unsatisfactory but none knowing why. It can be demoralizing for employees to be promoted into jobs from which several individuals have been laterally transferred, fired, or demoted. Employees become concerned about what elements in the job have changed in order to support their success. Extreme anxiety can develop among promotees into such jobs, who, fearing the failure their predecessors experienced, may quit before they too fail.

Workers are concerned about how their performance will be measured and what constitutes a job well done in concrete terms. They are sensitive to the visible accomplishments of those promoted. When they perceive that the best performers among them—best according to measurements they understand and respect—are being advanced, they feel that the promotion system is fair and that the criteria are being used justly.

Performance Criteria and Organization Values

That performance criteria must be compatible with each job almost goes without saying. That they must reflect organization values is less obvious. Many companies for example stress initiative and creativity as major criteria for advancement into jobs with decision-making responsibilities when in fact their real-life reward and punishment systems may not recognize or support these abilities. Thus the criteria purportedly used to evaluate performance actually have no place in the promotion scheme. The expectations that these misrepresented selection criteria create in the employee are never fulfilled.

There is evidence that performance in any work situation is consistant with the ability of the organization to recognize achievement and reward it. The promotion system must therefore be concerned with the development opportunities and enrichment potential in the work environment that are available to the employee. It must be especially sensitive to the capability of the existing work milieu to reinforce the achievement-oriented person. The employee who has been filling a job that is challenging and tough and that presents some risks also anticipates that the chances for visible rewards of success are equally available and will be consistent with his achievement.

The question of organization values weighs heavily on the methods that employees use to accomplish job objectives. The issue here is not adherence to corporate ethics, which is presumed, but conformity with certain styles of behavior that the company may prefer.

High-potential employees to whom corporations look for leadership occupy jobs that require adaptive and innovative behavior. Unstructured behavior, however, is often not supported by the corporate culture, which may attempt to control styles of action by taboos and social pressure. Performance criteria usually reflect these culture norms more than the relevant performance on a job. Therefore, a gap exists between the behavior the organization defines as productive and the behavior that reaches objectives. Promotions that reward achievements resulting from flexible behavior are more meaningful to the employee than those that recognize mimicry of established behavior patterns.

Performance Factors

Performance factors are categories of work activity to be measured. Performance criteria are measures, standards, or ways of evaluating work activity. *Factors* are what is to be measured; *criteria* are methods to measure those factors. Work activity is another way of describing on-the-job behavior since it is goal-oriented behavior (or activity) that is predictable.

Most performance appraisal systems used in American industry today are highly factor-oriented. These factors, which purport to describe performance, actually describe behavior on the job in terms of traditional items such as "Sense of responsibility" and "Attitude." Managerial and nonmanagerial performance appraisal systems are much alike except for degrees of depth in these factors.

Performance appraisal forms for production workers contain a series of factors such as "Attendance," "Tardiness," "Quality of work," and most include "Attitude." Appraisal methods for production and clerical jobs often use a numerical range for each factor. A range of 1 to 4 might indicate outstanding to failing performance. To evaluate attitude with such a scale is meaningless and has little impact on the employee for purposes of either development or discipline.

The major flaw in this system is that it emphasizes the how rather than the what—how the employee behaved in relation to job duties rather than what was accomplished as a result of the behavior. The implication is that acceptable productivity or performance is possible only through prescribed behavior. This is reinforced in many companies in production work and clerical positions, and it helps turn them into doomsday jobs. The consequences of this rigidity are that management finds it difficult to identify potential high performers and may use irrelevant if not arbitrary means of identifying promotable employees.

Performance Objectives

Managers argue that it is costly and impractical to create a different performance appraisal form for each job category. They argue that it is difficult to list more and more performance factors to define the parameters of a task.

They are correct on both counts. But the error in their argument is the assumption that human activity is unchanging and predetermined and thus can be reduced to a quantified scale of behaviors. Creating new performance factors of a special nature for every job is impossible. It is also unnecessary. It is fantasy to believe that a list of 10, 20, or even 100 words could describe the entire spectrum of relevant activity needed for job success.

The answer is that employee performance should be evaluated against specific job *objectives* to which the employee and the appraiser are both committed. Commitment is achieved when the employee participates in identifying and establishing objectives and is involved in deciding how performance should be measured. Participative analysis, problem solving, and decision making determine the extent of the employee's success in relation to the objective. It is from such analyses that practical and necessary development activities and organization weaknesses are identified and team-building efforts inaugurated.

Promotions that result from objective-oriented and participative appraisal systems have more value to the employee and contribute significantly to his need satisfaction and motivation. The employee gains a stake in his future because he is a party to it while the organization avoids paternalistic approaches to advancement.

This is not to say that behavior factors are worthless as indicators of employee performance but rather that they are secondary to the achievement of agreed-upon job objectives. Appraisal forms may include such items as "Attitude." To make them relevant the company should analyze what behavior is usually exhibited by a person with a "satisfactory" attitude. These behavior elements are then described in the appraisal form and reinforced on the job.

Because human activity is dynamic, appraisal criteria should be reviewed periodically. One way to do this is to analyze the individuals considered to be candidates for all promotions in the company over a period of a year or more. Their strengths and weaknesses should be listed, and rejected candidates should be compared with promotees. When differences are subtle or nonexistent or when the measurements used are not directly associated with prior or current work, there is the likelihood that certain of the criteria are no longer applicable. The appraisal elements should then be revised, with the participation of employees, as described. Thus the criteria for rewards are clarified, and promotions are readily seen as being achievements linked to known, practical expectations.

Salary and Promotion

Some companies do not give pay increases to management, clerical, and many sales people at the time of promotion. The implication is that the employee must prove himself in his new job just as he did on his old one. In this case money is both a lure and a reward.

The employee may have a general idea of how much money he will receive because he knows something about the compensation program. He will therefore not be surprised by the amount he receives. This does not mean he cannot be disappointed, particularly if he knows the latitudes that the compensation package allows. If he believes he deserves more money and knows that the compensation program would allow more, he is likely to feel cheated and may look for another job. If the increase is about what he expects, this reinforces his concept of the fairness of company practices, and he will tend to regard the extra salary as an appropriate amount. These dynamics also apply to both merit and annual increases when promotions are not involved.

In organizations where there is more secrecy about salary practices, expectations are less specific. An employee may still feel disappointed at not receiving a higher raise, but he has less knowledge of what his increase might be and is usually not so embittered when his expectations are not met.

When a surprisingly big increase in salary is received, there is a temporary moment of elation followed by curiosity, suspicion, fear, or even hostility. Some workers attempt to increase their output to justify the additional money. Thus the raise serves as a temporary motivator, but the stimulus is short-lived. Output will level off when the employee perceives that he is justifying his salary.

Some employees will react in a defensive manner to a big increase, feeling that their salary is too good to be true. They compare themselves with others in the organization whom they suspect or know earn as much as they or even less. They may see themselves as less deserving of these earnings than others. This leads them to become secretive about their work, fearing that if too many others know what they do and how, their relative lack of merit will be revealed. Fellow workers become a threat. Employees who consider themselves overpaid constantly fear their job content will be discovered not to justify the money.

Another aspect of raises associated with promotions is timing. A salary increase at the time of a promotion may serve as recognition for what has been accomplished or as a motivator in the form of payment in advance for accomplishments to come. A delay in an increase arouses curiosity. The employee looks for signs indicating the time is near. When much time passes, he feels let down or even cheated. He begins to feel underpaid and misused. The promotion begins to sour. He may have more work and greater responsibilities, but there is nothing in his pay envelope to show for it. "How much more proof do they need?" becomes a nagging question. The employee's internal clock tells him to move on.

Job Categories and Perceptions of Promotions

One form of motivation of course is competition for promotion. Promotions are used to stimulate competition more often with clerical, managerial, and sales workers than with employees in almost any other occupation category. Many competent and hardworking employees are not interested in promotions, however, because they perceive heated competition with fellow workers as being socially unacceptable, and social acceptance is an important issue within these occupation categories.

Technical workers, such as scientists, engineers, and researchers, reject promotions that remove them from their laboratories and experimental projects and force them into administrative and managerial duties. They do not respond to the usual motivation techniques, which they consider unnecessary. Their needs are sometimes satisfied through horizontal enrichment rather than vertical advancement.

In some job categories, however, promotions provide a deep sense of growth and development. When the work requires high degrees of specialization and where knowledge of the importance and magnitude of the job elicits personal involvement, promotions have considerable emotional impact. Workers responsible for massive turbines or complex, technologically advanced equipment, as in power plants, often react in this manner.

It is difficult for mass production jobs to provide this sense of development and concern. The same is true of lower-level staff positions, as in some large accounting departments, where every job is similar to the next. Promotions contain only subtle or slight self-actualizing elements for these categories of employees. When a promotion involves special company-sponsored training and development for them, its impact is greater.

Promotions and Professionalism

Promotions can have great value to workers striving for professionalism. *Professionalism* has come to mean *uncommon,* a quality not everybody can achieve. It implies skills, expertise, personal and occupational development. It indicates challenge, lofty purpose, and special ethics (whether real or imagined). Professionalism provides status, gives the worker a feeling of identity and even exclusiveness, and satisfies ego and social needs. These need satisfiers often surpass the lure of increased wages.

Employees who have managed to retain jobs in high-paying glamour industries (electronics, aerospace, computer) or services (management consulting, ecology, advertising) despite a shallow base of marketable expertise also seek professionalism on the job and off. This is done by joining professional associations, to which they pay handsome dues. They typically work toward restrictive prerequisites and limited membership in an effort to define their own positions more clearly. Promotions are important to these people when they enhance job knowledge, provide status, and broaden existing skills. Their professional self-image is further reinforced by social recognition.

Personal Aspirations and Perceptions of Promotions

Each person brings to a job a set of aspirations and expectations that are influenced by his prior successes or failures and that define his sense of achievement. Behavior on the job is a function of these influences.

Promotions are strongly linked to the employee's level of aspirations because they betoken success. But it cannot be assumed that all workers perceive success in the same way. Promotion systems that fail to accommodate different success norms may fail to meet the achievement needs of employees.

It is not always possible to equate objective achievement with feelings of success. If an individual's aspiration levels are low, it will take relatively little performance to make him feel successful. On the other hand a piece of work recognized by peers and superiors as an achievement will not seem a howling success to the worker who expects more of himself.

Employees who have minimal or even low expectations of success but who obtain promotions experience high levels of satisfaction, although those whose lower-order needs—survival and safety—are paramount may not feel the additional work and responsibility that come with promotion are worth the threat to those needs. Those whose expectations are high on the contrary may experience dissatisfaction with an advancement. These reactions are a function of self-esteem and of feelings about one's potential, capabilities, or status.

Failure to achieve promotion or the anxiety that a promotion will not be given will often cause a worker to protect his self-esteem by blaming the system, his tools, poor communication, or other factors outside his control. He may alienate himself or cut the ties between himself and the results of his work. In anticipation of failure he can clearly delineate who is responsible for what. With promotion he will no longer reject the relationship between himself and the results of his work. The emotional effects of the desire for promotion are similar to those of the need for social recognition or love.

Two Case Histories

A few examples will illustrate the effect that expectations and aspirations have on an employee's reaction to a promotion.

Mr. A sets lofty goals for himself. He has experienced a series of successes at previous job levels, and his aspirations are high. His expectations of what he will get in terms of intangible and tangible rewards are also high. His job is a difficult one, but Mr. A's attitude makes it seem attractive and even inviting. Mr. A is confident, he anticipates the future. He does not fear controversy, and he is willing to take reasonable risks. He seeks success so much that he sometimes sets goals he cannot be sure he will reach.

Mr. B, on the other hand, has no lofty ideas about his job. He knows it is a tough one. He claims to be a realist and often states, "If I can bat .500, I'm happy." He took his present job after achieving only marginal success in another field. Mr. B hopes to avoid failure more than he strives for success. For him success is simply not failing. Therefore, he is delighted when his performance appraisal is delayed a week because he insists, "What I don't know won't hurt me." Unlike Mr. A he will not set his own goals; he prefers to pursue established ones. His expectations are modest because he has learned that you win a few and you lose a few and that rewards are given accordingly. Mr. B plans for tomorrow but spends little time gambling on the future. He is terrified of new projects because he does not know what to expect and is unable to anticipate the result of the project or superiors' reaction to it. However, what he does he does well.

Mr. A is promoted because of his courage, his imagination, and the vigor with which he pursues objectives he seems destined to reach. Mr. B is promoted because of his steadiness, accuracy, attention to detail, and solidity. Although he is not an imaginative person or one to take risks, his conservative approach lends stability to the overall staff.

Within a short time after their promotions, *both are quitting!*

Both perceive that in their new positions they are being forced into behavior they cannot accommodate and are losing control over their destinies. They have suddenly become subject to the organization's definition of success and failure, the organization's evaluation of their respective abilities to contribute, and the organization's best judgment about their usefulness. Both therefore see these new assignments as doomsday jobs.

One of the problems Mr. A has on the new job is that he never knows for sure where he stands. He receives insufficient feedback from his boss and his peers. Accepting Mr. A's previous success as "only natural," his boss has failed to satisfy Mr. A's need to hear about his own success. Mr. A refuses to continue in that situation. The raise he has gotten is in his opinion nice but not enough to show. The new job gives him somewhat more latitude in decision making than he had before, but Mr. A is willing to stick his neck out on big decisions provided he can apply his skill and talent to the task. Being given that opportunity would be its own reward. On his new job, however, he perceives too many important areas over which he will have little or no control.

Mr. A is quitting because he is disappointed.

On Mr. B's first day on the job to which he has been promoted, his boss visited him and proudly set the stage for the future. Mr. B has proved himself sufficiently in the short time he has been there and is now being allowed to set his own objectives. He will of course be expected to report on his achievements weekly (later monthly) and will have the benefit of immediate feedback. Planning of course will be an important part of his job, and he is expected to prepare modest forecasts of results and commit himself to them. As his boss left Mr. B's office, he laughed and said, "Go, go, go, young man! It's a dog-eat-dog world out there, and promotions don't grow on trees. Go get 'em, tiger!"

Mr. B heaves a sigh of relief when he decides to quit after so desperately wanting to retain his employment. He is out from under.

Implications for Selection

The saga of Messrs. A and B points up some critical issues. More rigorous evaluation is needed at the time of screening for promotion in order to move beyond the stage of simply discovering a person's success or failure. It is more important to understand *why* an employee has succeeded or failed.

Candidates for promotion who have recently experienced success are confident and even aggressive. Their expectations of future success are high. Those who have experienced a major setback, recall a series of failures, or who simply cannot identify clear-cut examples of personal success may be ambivalent in their reaction to the challenge of the proposed advancement. They often hesitate to take risks and respond to performance review questions in a manner that lacks confidence.

The culture of the organization must be analyzed objectively as well to insure the compatibility of employee needs with the available satisfiers on the new job. This accommodation is a realistic recognition that an organization's atmosphere and the resulting precedents, traditions, and systems of reward and punishment may be supportive to some but defeating to others.

The work group or department into which a worker is promoted can influence motivation and affect the way he perceives and responds to the promotion. Every group has its special norms of behavior that its members are expected to abide by. Those who do not are isolated from in-group relationships and may experience interpersonal conflicts with other members. To the worker who seeks achievement through reasonable risk taking, decision making, and hard work, a close working association with a group of sophisticated cynics and self-appointed corporate critics can mean anguish. To the failure-avoiding Lt. Pulvers of the corporate world, who select goals they are sure to achieve and do just enough work to avoid risks and attention, association with a group of rate busters is anathema. To both, the jobs into which they have been promoted rapidly become millstones, and the resulting sense of doom may impel them to resign.

Many companies are amazed to learn how high their turnover rates are among those promoted six to twelve months before termination. While there may be some involuntary terminations due to inability to perform the work, voluntary quits are more prevalent and surely more dramatic. Sometimes the reason is pay, as described earlier. But often it is a feeling of inadequacy and confusion that may be difficult to express. Data should be collected on the turnover rate of those promoted so that the organization can analyze what influences—from the employee's personal makeup, from the work milieu, or from unforeseeable or unavoidable events—have caused this doubly damaging waste of manpower.

Limitations on Promotion Systems

Circumstances arising from the nature of the business macrocosm hinder the promotion process in many companies. Union contracts operate on the principle of seniority. Promotions for outstanding work alone are rarely possible. Many foreman's jobs are filled by college graduates who restrict the advancement of factory workers.

Even if promotion opportunities were less restricted for factory workers, it would be difficult for management to measure differences in workers' potential ability accurately. Most production jobs offer limited opportunities for initiative or problem solving and decision making beyond a narrow scope. Jobs are routinized and highly structured. The docile, unimaginative worker who does what he is told and works by the numbers is rated as the good worker.

The creative production worker, who might have strong potential in less structured and more challenging work assignments, is the one who represents the greatest loss to the company that cannot promote him.

He is less likely to be satisfied with rigid work routines; he is more easily bored and more likely to be alienated. He will probably seek an outlet for his needs in union activities as a steward or a member of the union executive committee. If these avenues are not open to him, he may quit his job—through no fault of the company.

For many production workers "advancement" may be horizontal rather than vertical. For example, while seniority may restrict the worker from rapid upward advancement, horizontal shifts to a better job may be possible. In this frame of reference, *better* means cleaner, less strenuous, or less dangerous.

The pattern of corporate life today also makes it difficult to identify managerial success or failure. The average worker is a part of an organic human network of interdependent functions. He rarely achieves or fails alone. Managers who consistently work through groups, task forces, committees, and project teams cannot claim sole merit for success.

As noted at the beginning of the chapter, organizations with multiple layers of management may advance promising employees by half-steps, so that they are merely continuing junior-level responsibilities on a more senior level with only subtle changes in scope. In a large number of organizations, the assistant—the employee at the next level under the senior manager—serves three major functions: (1) He performs work delegated by the senior manager, (2) he performs the tasks that constitute the core of the junior position, and (3) he receives training for the senior position. When this pattern is reenacted on subsequent layers down through the organization, channels for advancement can become clogged, and blocked mobility results.

Lack of Management Support

Many companies with potentially excellent promotion processes find that the system is not actively supported by management. Managers may accept the program passively, protecting their best and offering expendables for promotion. This behavior is indicative of defensive and monopolistic attitudes and a lack of understanding about the objectives of the promotion system. It also signifies lack of team-building efforts. It is frequently found when the promotion system has been developed without the involvement of line management in the early stages and when the company has no human resources or organization development programs.

Underdevelopment and underutilization of people assumes an unchanging work flow, stationary technological levels, fixed financial circumstances, and unvarying individual career objectives and personal needs. This leads to a lack of advancement potential and results in outside recruitment to fill key jobs in the organization. Outside recruitment in turn robs the promotion system of credibility, weakens motivation, and forces the training function to become skills-oriented in a narrow sense. The cycle is thus perpetuated, hurting morale, particularly among high-potential workers, and giving the organization a poor reputation as a career-stifling company.

The effect of promoting expendables is equally damaging. Those who are more highly qualified do not receive the recognition they deserve and are passed by in favor of underqualified or failure-avoiding people. In addition those who are promoted may know that they are thought of, correctly or incorrectly, as expendables, which drains them of the self-confidence and motivation they need to operate effectively. This may lead to discharge for inability to do the work or resignation because of anxiety, frustration, and stress.

Management support of the promotion system is therefore vital not only to the success of the advancement program itself but to the maintenance of high performance in the present body of employees and the company's ability to attract manpower in the future. The organization can insure this support by including all management functions in the formation and administration of the promotion program and by developing candidates for advancement through ongoing training, development, and vestibule programs.

The Need to Advance

Advancement needs have a strong cultural foundation in the United States, where traditions of class, title, and nobility do not interfere with occupational mobility as they do in some countries. Middle-class values in America teach children that their opportunities will be limited only by the degree of their determination, imagination, hard work, and know-how, although sociologists find that the underprivileged are likely to be more content with less success than children from middle-class families. Education is seen as the vehicle by which success is possible.

Promotions in an organization are structured signs of recognition. Workers seek promotions as rewards for achievement. When a promotion is accompanied by a salary increase or the promise of one, an intimate system of personal values is affected. The significance of the advancement is evaluated by the employee in terms of visible upward movement on the organization chart, which satisfies ego needs and assures peer recognition. Fulfillment and feelings of accomplishment, self-confidence, and reinforcement of behavior patterns are the end products of a good promotion system.

TEN

a turnover action program

No COMPANY's turnover problem can be solved until managers and supervisors from the top to the lowest possible level are aware of the factors that create doomsday jobs, understand their own roles in perpetuating them, and are committed to eradicating them. As long as management sees turnover in any other light—as strictly a concern of personnel or industrial relations, as the responsibility only of the foremen, as the behavior of workers who were undesirable anyway—the problem will never be solved.

This is not to say that the staff units primarily engaged in employment and labor relations forfeit their functions. To the contrary, as the following discussion will show, the success of a turnover action program depends heavily on their activities to provide the entire organization with information and feedback, monitor progress, and serve as the axis for the turnover task forces described in Chapter 2.

Turnover action of this dimension constitutes a critical intervention by the organization into its own processes for the purpose of bringing about change. It entails an ongoing effort if the change is to take root and permanently displace the conditions that lead to turnover. A one-shot project can produce feelings of insecurity and distrust of management and raise charges of tampering, paternalism, and hip shooting. One-shot approaches rarely produce worthwhile results or sustain the organization renewal that is the ultimate purpose of the turnover action program.

A caution about change should be kept in mind. It is difficult if not impossible to isolate or contain meaningful change. Organization interrelationships are complex and sensitive. A chain reaction of change is typical. Changing an organization's size, skill mix, objectives, or reward and punishment system results in other changes, some of which are unexpected.

These unplanned but equally important transformations that occur may pass unnoticed because only the planned change is observed. For example, a modification of a production or assembly process may improve working conditions for some employees, but the conflict and frustration it generates in others may be ignored because sensitivities are tunneled toward the planned change. It is unwise to plan for change without preparing for additional changes and guarding against injurious side effects.

The turnover action plan that is the heart of this chapter makes planned change and continuing alertness to its consequences part of every manager's concern. It incorporates turnover results into the management process—whatever the basic managerial job assignment—in terms of not only manpower inventory and forecasts but also managers' performance appraisals. The plan is presented in outline form for ready adaptation to each organization's size, business, and environment. The objective of this approach is to translate the turnover problem into operational terms that have practical meaning for line managers and staff executives as well.

Whose Responsibility Is Turnover?

For the most part turnover is thought of as wholly a personnel or industrial relations problem. This is a tragic fallacy. Personnel and industrial relations are support services to line management. Except for the employees who work in these areas, they are nonproduction staff functions. Their heads typically lack line operating authority and are given neither the power base nor the mandate to effect change directly. Their role is to share responsibility with operating management for turnover by virtue of their overlapping interests and functions. The following is a list of exclusive and mutual responsibilities in connection with turnover that rest in operating management and industrial relations staff members.

Industrial Relations Managers | Line Managers

Jointly develop appropriate job descriptions and specifications and consult on salary classifications.

Industrial Relations Managers	Line Managers
	Requisition new hires according to specific needs in keeping with job descriptions.
Gain workable understandings about the manpower needs of line management.	
Monitor requisitions made by line managers to insure compatibility with the job description, salary scale, and function of the vacated job.	
Conduct economical and effective recruitment campaign.	
Insure that screening mechanisms— interviewing, reference verifications, tests, and other prescreening devices —are performed by qualified personnel in a valid and objective manner.	

Provide training for members of the employment function and line management in effective interviewing, test analysis, and preemployment screening techniques.

Industrial Relations Managers	Line Managers
	Interview in an objective, professional manner. Base hiring decisions on valid criteria in keeping with guidelines learned in training.
Collect data necessary to monitor the effectiveness of the management process; evaluate feedback in communications loops; conduct turnover analysis and salary surveys in house and in the community; evaluate advancement systems; analyze the state of labor relations; review personnel policy, procedures, and practices; and team-build by initiating involvement, commitment, concern, and action with respect to modifications.	

Cooperate in the analysis, development, and implementation of a mutually acceptable and relevant performance appraisal system.

	Practice effective management styles and techniques to insure maximum utilization and motivation of employees and provide opportunities for participation and occupational development.
Consult with operating management to enlist support for research and determine the causes of inadequate control over turnover.	

Provide relevant training programs and development systems at all levels of the organization, keeping in mind that training and development cannot be exclusively industrial relations or line management programs if they are to gain any measure of success.

	Attend and encourage attendance at training programs. Use the training experience in daily operations, and insure that it is reinforced down the line.
Act as catalysts in bringing together appropriate functional elements in the organization to operate in a team mode, regardless of how diverse	

Industrial Relations Managers	Line Managers
team participation may be, if the combined expertise of the team members can contribute to framing and eventually solving organization problems.	
Persistently work toward the inclusion of manpower planning inventory and forecast data into the management decision-making process. This includes turnover statistics and costs as a part of the financial reporting system.	
Bring to the attention of upper managers the facts necessary for them to become aware of the complexity and scope of the problems facing the organization, and provide sufficient data to elicit analysis and functional creativeness to insure that action will follow.	
	Include all employees in the turnover feedback loop in a participative way and enlist their support through leveling communications techniques.

Turnover Action Plan

The model for a turnover action plan that follows divides the implementation of change into 12 phases. Phases 5, 6, and 7 may be undertaken simultaneously for total saturation or introduced serially, as desired. The plan is intended to reach into every echelon of the organization's human resources, providing a network of mutually supportive interrelationships that vitalize the entire functional organism.

The system that is created as a result of making turnover the manager's job emphasizes participative objective setting; communication and feedback as a function of human-oriented leadership; and motivation in the form of recognition, authority, responsibility, and the satisfaction of achievement needs. It also provides important team-building experiences for the organization. In this way it is possible to rid the company of values and systems that force managers into disguising or avoiding problems and to reduce or eliminate the circumstances that perpetuate doomsday jobs.

Phase 1. Getting a Handle on the Problem

Who: Industrial relations and personnel.
Supported by: Payroll and systems.
What: Frame the turnover problem and measure its scope and intensity.

1. Obtain top management's support for an ongoing study of turnover with the objective of reducing costs (or maintaining current favorable turnover trends) and maximizing human potential.
2. Develop a workable system by which to collect and record data on personnel movements weekly and/or monthly under the headings of promotion, transfer, demotion, discharge, involuntary retirement, layoffs, leaves of absence, and personal reasons.
3. Assign these responsibilities to members of the personnel or industrial relations department as a permanent part of job responsibilities and as one of the factors on which performance will be based.
4. Implement a statistical study of turnover.
5. Calculate percentages of turnover, expansion rates, and voluntary and involuntary turnover rates, and develop trend summaries and statistical analyses.
6. Derive census totals based upon the total head count in all divisions and departments and compute the net changes in population for all payroll classifications. Develop these figures for each section, department, division, and reporting location.
7. Develop trend charts and other visual representations to display the problem in its full scope.
8. Track turnover monthly.
9. Develop quarterly, semi-annual, and annual statistical summaries.
10. Distribute a monthly statistical report to all members of the top-management team, accompanying the report with a written analysis of trends and preliminary assumptions concerning causes of turnover.
11. Hold monthly meetings with top management to measure the scope of the problem and sustain interest.
12. Give copies of the data to be discussed at the meeting to all members of the top-management decision-making team in advance. Couch the presentation in nonaccusatory terms so that it does not arouse defensiveness.

Phase 2. Turnover Costs

Who: Industrial relations and personnel.
Supported by: Finance, accounting, directors of all major cost centers, regional managers, and local plant managers.
What: Calculate the cost of turnover to the company in dollars.

1. Identify all categories of tangible costs associated with hiring and termination as discussed in Chapter 5.
2. Assess the feasibility of accounting for the costs of intangible losses.

3. Determine what known cost figures are readily available and for what periods.
4. If cost data are not available in the categories desired, request the needed cost breakdowns from operating units.
5. Record the number of all hires and terminations for each reporting unit, and record known costs in each of the cost categories.
6. Develop cost totals monthly, quarterly, semiannually, and annually.
7. Present cost data to the top-management decision-making group with a clear explanation of all assumptions and limitations. Use charts, tables, and other visual aids to demonstrate the costs incurred by the organization. Make sure that materials are available for distribution.
8. Translate the data into descriptive statements as in the following examples. The number of people who left the company during the first quarter of the year was equal to one-fourth of our current total number of employees. The cost of terminations during the first quarter exceeded the combined profits of ABC and XYZ departments. It costs 3.75 times more to fire or lay off an employee than to hire one. It costs 2.60 times more to hire and fire an employee in our San Francisco office than in our Toledo operation.
9. Ask top management to set acceptable cost limits.
10. Formalize the cost limits in terms of reasonable objectives through the current year. These levels should be considered a first cut at the problem rather than a management mandate.
11. Isolate areas where costs and turnover are highest and where more concentrated effort should perhaps be made.
12. Begin to brainstorm feasible ways to analyze the problem further in order to provide management with additional options.

Phase 3. Data Correlation

Who: Industrial relations and personnel.
Supported by: Systems, data processing, district and/or regional managers, local plant managers, and industrial relations, representatives in the field.
What: Begin to explore the causes of turnover.

1. Develop manual, semi-automated, or computerized systems for correlating the personal and occupational characteristics of exiting employees with reasons for termination.
2. Track experience to determine frequency.
3. Communicate findings in verbal, statistical, and visual form to top management.
4. Communicate findings to interviewers, placement analysts, and

managers at all ranks who have authority to hire, fire, promote, and assign work.
5. Establish a monthly schedule for collecting, correlating, and analyzing data and issuing reports.
6. Consolidate data correlations each month with the new turnover experience of divisions, departments, and the company as a whole.

Phase 4. Management Mandate

Who: Chief executive officer.
Supported by: Top executive group responsible for corporate policy and decision making.
What: Makes a commitment to solving the turnover problem and initiates action.

1. Formally announces the reduction of turnover as one of the top corporate objectives for the year.
2. Issues directives to heads of line divisions to begin analyzing the causes of turnover in their respective operating areas and calls for monthly progress reports of activities. Indicates general expectations without imposing artificial objectives or problem-solving methods on them.
3. Instructs industrial relations and personnel to act in a support capacity and supplies division heads with all available data.
4. Directs personnel and industrial relations to establish as many task forces or study groups as may be needed to review the company's posture with respect to all employee relations programs: employment opportunities, compensation, benefits, training, management development, promotion systems and performance appraisal methods, and so forth. Directs the inclusion of both line and staff people in these task forces.
5. Provides each task force or study group with an overall mission as a guide to be elaborated upon or modified as these groups deem necessary. Assigns target dates for preliminary, intermediate, and target briefings and conferences.

Phase 5. Task Force Organization

Who: Industrial relations and personnel.
What: Insure that task forces are formed and prepared for action.

1. Give detailed briefings on the turnover problem to division heads, and provide operating guidelines to be used only until divisions and task forces are functioning effectively and can design their own operating structures.
2. Work through division heads to obtain the names of line managers who will serve on joint staff-line task forces.

3. Assign industrial relations and personnel employees to these task forces on the basis of the employees' specific expertise and current jobs.
4. Send the ranking relations and/or personnel officers to the initial meeting of each task force. Request others in top management to recognize each task force formally and to indicate support, reiterate needs, and outline opportunities and objectives.

Phase 6. Task Force Activation
Who: Each task force.
What: Meets to plan its objectives and approaches.

1. Elects a chairman.
2. Assigns responsibility for taking minutes at each meeting to a member of the task force, such minutes to be sent to the head of industrial relations or personnel, top executives, and each task force member.
3. Establishes a meeting schedule and reserves a conference or meeting room for this purpose.
4. Analyzes the objective of its mission, and brainstorms its assigned aspect of the turnover problem.
5. At each subsequent meeting, modifies its objectives as needed to define its work more precisely.
6. Develops milestones for itself and performance criteria on which it agrees to be judged.
7. Conducts research and investigations as needed between meetings to develop facts.
8. Evaluates and summarizes such facts at the next meeting.
9. Periodically reexamines its definition of the problem and the validity of its findings.
10. Ultimately develops recommendations for consideration by top management and problem-solving groups headed by division heads.

Phase 7. Line Management Organization and Activation
Who: Each division head, followed by each subordinate-level manager in the division.
Supported by: Operating managers at all levels below the conference leader's.
What: Meets with subordinate managers to organize the effective managerial action.

Note: The techniques in phase 7 are repeated at each managerial level, beginning with the highest-ranking manager or executive in the line division (called "division head") and ending with the lowest level of management in the division. A series of meetings is held at each level.

1. Introduces the subject of turnover by reviewing the reason for the meeting and presenting the corporate turnover objective. Summarizes and frames the problem, indicating cost-profit relationships and describing the effect of turnover on operating efficiency, and makes certain that all members of the group have an understanding of the report. Leads the group in seeking ways to reduce turnover in the division and to provide all managers with means of dealing with the problem.
2. Elicits the participation and commitment of each member of the group in an unrestricted atmosphere of objective problem solving.
3. Turns the early meetings into brainstorming sessions to generate ideas about the causes of turnover. No criticism or in-depth comment on the ideas is offered. All ideas are written on a blackboard or chart pads. If pads are used the sheets are taped to the walls of the meeting room before the meeting. Quantity, not quality, of ideas is desired. The group works in a total vacuum, untouched or uninfluenced by reality. The conference leader acts only as recorder and takes no leadership role. In addition he does not guide the group toward a solution. Concepts, philosophies, precedents, and personal status are not at stake. All ideas are recorded, and none are rejected.
4. Guides the group at a subsequent meeting to frame the turnover problem by drafting a first statement of objectives based upon the original corporate concept developed by the top-management decision-making group.
5. Leads the group to problem solving through its evaluation of all brainstormed ideas recorded earlier. Each idea is examined in an open atmosphere to test how it "fits," what its consequences might be, and how it stands up when weighed against other ideas. The group then assesses whether the ideas apply to companywide turnover, and then it ranks the ideas by priority.
6. Leads the group to rewrite its objective on the basis of how it now feels about the problem with emphasis on measurable criteria of accomplishment. A broad statement of purpose or intent is included, and conceptualized statements about how the objective will be reached in terms of group action, change, implementation, monitoring, and ongoing maintenance are incorporated.
7. Participates in the group's attempts to reach consensus about the ideas it has been discussing. Some will be rejected; new ones may

be proposed and accepted; new priorities may be assigned. At this point the group must agree to disagree and not be fragmented or disappointed by conflict and differences of opinion. Expressions of personal attitudes are invited and evaluated for their effectiveness or ineffectiveness as foundations for management styles. As decisions are reached on the most likely causes of turnover, individual motivation and group cohesiveness begin to emerge. The result is a list of causes of turnover ranked in order of significance and representing the group's best judgment of the situation.
8. Helps the group to categorize the ideas on the basis of the priorities assigned. For example several ideas may be put under the heading of "Employee Compensation, Recognition, and Rewards." Another category might be "Policies: Their Administration and Implementation." Still another might be "Special Problems Resulting from Lack of Managerial Training and Development." When the first categorization is completed, the list of ideas should be reviewed again for relevance and ideas combined when it is reasonable to do so.

Phase 8. Conference on Progress I

Who: Top executive decision-making group, division heads, and task force chairmen.
What: Meet to review progress.

1. Evaluate progress and approaches, resolve basic conflicts, eliminate duplications of effort, insure that task forces are supportive of line efforts, and check that all research data are being shared with all participants. Assign to task forces the responsibility for staff work as needed by the various divisions in their problem-solving sessions.
2. Summarize all ideas, approaches, problems, needs, and opportunities identified by each task force and division head. Categorize and assign priorities to the entire list.
3. Review the corporate turnover objective and revise it if need be according to recommendations submitted by division heads and task force chairmen.

Phase 9. Line Management Evaluation

Who: Each division head, followed by each subordinate-level manager in the division.
Supported by: Operating managers at all levels below the conference leader's.
What: Meets with subordinate managers to evaluate division concepts, methods, and progress.

1. Leads the group to evaluate its perspective, its progress, and the compatibility of its objectives with the revised corporate objectives in the light of facts and inputs obtained during the phase 8 conference. The group makes reasonable revisions where needed but with the focus on the problems within the division.
2. Has the group brainstorm to develop general solutions for each category of turnover causes, using the techniques indicated in phase 7. The group does not address individual items under each category but restricts itself to formulating solutions for each broad category.
3. Lists each approach suggested, and calls on the group to evaluate its good and bad consequences. All ideas are ranked according to how effectively they might solve the turnover problem by correcting each category of causes with the fewest adverse consequences. These alternatives should identify in broad terms the actions needing to be taken.
4. Leads the group in further brainstorming sessions to apply the general solution to the individual items within each category. In so doing the group proposes practical ways of solving each problem within each category. The result is a series of steps consistent with the general solution. Consider the following examples:

Broad Category	Brainstorming Results
Employee Compensation, Recognition, and Rewards	The entire compensation program should be upgraded, expanded, and liberalized, and new incentives should be introduced.
(a) Employees are underpaid at the time of hire.	A wage survey of similar companies and jobs in the immediate labor market should be conducted to determine comparative levels.
(b) Insufficient raises are given, at too infrequent intervals.	Salary increase policies should be reviewed to determine why the rates of increase are so low and the intervals so lengthy.
(c) Employees are not paid enough money at the time of promotion.	The promotion policy and related pay-increase practices should be reviewed, and raises with promotions should be increased.
(d) There are no other means available of recognizing outstanding contribution except annual increases or promotions.	New forms of recognition should be adopted—for example, extra vacation days and department awards.

5. Leads the group to consider the advantages and disadvantages of all the solutions suggested to solve each turnover problem identified and to select those with the fewest adverse effects.
6. Elicits the group's predictions in general terms of the outcome after each of the solutions is applied to each of the problems. The group also estimates the costs of implementing the solution. For example, the cost to the company of increasing starting salaries should be considered.
7. Helps the group review its broad categories and individual causes of turnover as well as its solutions and to rearrange them under three new headings: external, internal, and shared. External items deal with factors outside the division's control that are suspected of causing turnover. Examples would be company policies, compensation regulations, and vacation practices. Internal items would include division management and supervisory styles, delegation practices, discipline and supervisory interpretation of division or section rules, and performance appraisal methods. Shared items include activities within the division that require major support from external groups, such as training, employment recruitment and interviewing, and equipment maintenance.
8. Has the group indicate the department and the individual or individuals (in terms of job titles) primarily responsible for each item listed in the external, internal, and shared categories.
9. Leads the group in reviewing its objectives and determining compatibility with actions suggested to date. Makes changes where necessary in approach and brings objectives into sharper focus on the basis of what is now known about the problem.

Phase 10. Conference on Progress II

Who: Top executive decision-making group, division heads, and task force chairmen.
What: Meet to review progress.

1. Evaluate progress to date, resolve basic conflicts, and eliminate duplications of effort.
2. List, review, and rank categories of external turnover causes in order of priority.
3. Assign external causes to appropriate task forces already working in comparable areas. This approach gives the task forces practical input, provides a broader base of support and involvement, and reconfirms the need for solutions.

Phase 11. Creating the Problem-Solving Network

Who: Each division head and each subordinate-level manager in the division.

Supported by: Operating managers at all levels below the group leader's.

What: Meets with subordinates to redefine problems and objectives in operational terms and communicates with other division groups in a problem-solving network.

Note: Each manager responsible for a subordinate level of managers and supervisors is assigned the responsibility of heading up a problem-solving group of these subordinates. These groups are formed in order to gain the best judgments of their members and to broaden the base of involvement in and support for the turnover action program.

1. Organizes the problem-solving group, which devotes its early meetings to redefining problems and objectives.
2. Works with the group to uncover opportunities for action, and transmits group recommendations to the next higher division group. The division head in turn reports to top management through subsequent conferences on progress.
3. Brings the group feedback on the results of its recommendations and on the steps being taken to correct external and shared causes of turnover.

Phase 12. Evaluation of Progress and Outcomes

Who: Each problem-solving group.

Supported by: All subordinate groups in the division.

What: Establishes target dates, predicts outcomes, and determines means of appraising individual, group, and division accomplishment.

1. Brainstorms to find ways of evaluating and recognizing progress toward objectives that will be achieved by the division-level group and the subordinate problem-solving groups.
2. Assigns a series of target dates—for implementation of the solution, intermediate reports, and achievement—to each internal cause of turnover or adopts those established by the problem-solving group at the next higher level. Each member makes a personal commitment to the group target dates and in so doing develops his own pretarget-date schedule, pending review and approval by subordinate managers or supervisors.
3. Makes reasonable estimates of the effect each specific remedy should have on the turnover rate. In evaluations of the effectiveness of each problem-solving group, the remedies, or actions planned, are as important as the projected percentage of turnover reduction.

4. Establishes reasonable criteria, by which all group members agree to be held accountable, for measuring efforts to achieve objectives. This provides a sense of proprietorship in the total program while establishing turnover results as a part of the management performance appraisal process.

Another dimension can be added to the turnover action program: Supervisors can hold problem-solving meetings with employees for the purpose of indicating management's concern about turnover and its interest in improving the work environment for the individual. Recognition of the employee is made possible along with important ego-building and enrichment opportunities.

In order to realize the full potential of the program, a feedback network should be established so that the employee group receives information about the acceptability of its suggestions through various management strata to the top executive level.

The Interplay of Motivation and Achievement

The processes activated by the turnover action program unfold motivation factors. When the employees understand what is expected of them—what will constitute success or achievement—and when they have a share in developing these criteria, they likewise have a share in the outcome of the program. This stands as the basis of job security and provides work tasks that satisfy survival needs. Moreover, when employees themselves help decide how their achievement should be measured and actually participate in appraisals of their performance, they become more certain about the fairness of decisions. They know the rules of the road because they helped write them.

The need to belong, to achieve acceptance by and recognition from a work group, is satisfied through working with others toward objectives. Mutual support gratifies important social drives. Motivation likewise results from the self-confidence and status, the recognition and responsibility that spring from the work itself. When employees strive to attain a known objective that they have helped develop and are offered the means by which to achieve something worthwhile, ego needs begin to be met.

Finally, realizing one's own potential as a result of achieving objectives begins to satisfy self-fulfillment needs. Sometimes, knowing the channels for such exist, even though full actualization may be elusive, is strongly sustaining.

The achievements of business are a measure of its investment in human activity and the result of energies dedicated to meeting its objectives. Business exists because people want it to exist and contribute to its maintenance. Business therefore channels and focuses human talent, initiative, and know-how. Without the human factor the organization ceases to exist. When business fails to accommodate human endeavor, it defies its reason for being.

postscript

look to the future

EMPLOYMENT FUNCTIONS and department line operations using manpower planning techniques are those that will ultimately have the most realistic concept of corporate needs. The manpower planning approach provides important data about the company's manpower capabilities now and in the future. Divided into two phases, manpower inventory and manpower forecast, it objectively and systematically measures where the company stands in relation to its corporate objectives and what must be done to achieve the manpower posture necessary to make the objectives a reality.

The manpower inventory assesses the capabilities of the current staff by analyzing employees' education background, age, sex, performance, and other vital factors, including the number of people in each occupation and job grade. Workers are then evaluated in terms of ability to function effectively in current, lateral, and advanced positions. When attrition and the company's capability of developing and training its manpower are taken into account, future shortages are rapidly identified, and manpower forecasts can be drawn up.

The manpower planning approach has numerous beneficial ramifications. Matching the data against organization charts reveals blockages that could result in turnover among high-potential manpower. The inventory also helps the organization evaluate its ability to meet its obligation to provide employees with the training and achievement opportunities that prevent the creation and maintenance of doomsday jobs. When vacancies occur that cannot be filled from within the company, it is possible to bring people into the organization who not only fill its immediate needs but fit into its long-range goals. Job requisitions can be evaluated to determine the depth of experience, level of education, career objectives, and capacity for development required of applicants.

Thus the manpower planning approach enables the organization to select the person for the job who will be ready to assume greater responsibilities when the time comes because of the company's ability to utilize, train, and develop employees effectively and to forecast its needs in relation to its markets and the economy at large.

The overview provided by manpower planning data can be broadened and sharpened through an analysis of the organization, using a business status inventory. The following is an example of one that works well when administered by an impartial task force or study group devoted to the evaluation of opportunities for organization renewal and revitalization. Fully investigated and answered, these questions bring to light important strengths and weaknesses within the organization and help management focus on the tragedy of human underutilization in doomsday jobs.

Business Status Inventory [1]

1. Does the company have stated profit or operations objectives?
2. Who knows about these objectives?
3. Who should know about them? Who does not?
4. If the objectives have not been written, has a target date been set for drafting them?
5. If the company has such statements, were they met last year?
6. Were they met in any of the last five years?
7. Were they met comfortably or by a narrow margin?
8. If they were not met or only barely met, what are the reasons?
9. Describe in words, not figures from the financial statement, the financial situation of the company today.
10. Describe in words the outlook of the company for this year, the next three years, and the next five years.
11. List five key opportunities and needs of the company that if not met can prevent the accomplishment of the profit or operations objectives this year, next year, and within the next three years. Consider for inclusion labor needs, technological advances, research and development possibilities, new markets, and capital needs.
12. What formal plans have been developed to circumvent some or all of these problems?
13. What changes in business technology might affect the business organization in the next year and within the next three to five years?

---

[1] Adapted from D. B. Peskin, *The Building Blocks of EEO* (New York: World Publishing Company, 1971), pp. 27–31.

14. How will such changes affect the present workforce in terms of skills mix?
15. How will they affect the profit outlook?
16. If several of your most valued managers, top executives, or most skilled technicians were permanently unavailable, how would this affect the short-run success of the business?
17. How would it affect the long-run success of the business?
18. What action does this suggest?
19. What are your key labor markets or sources of employees?
20. What caliber of employee is most usually attracted to your business?
21. Evaluate the difficulty of finding employees with the skills you need, the training period required for them, any learning curve problems, and the salaries of skilled, semiskilled, and unskilled workers, and then analyze these factors for all payroll classifications of employees in order to begin to develop a manpower profile.
22. In how many of the last five years have you considered your labor markets to be satisfactory?
23. What plans have been made to gain a better share of the labor market for the company?
24. In what ways does the business maintain competitive rate scales?
25. In what ways does the company provide greater responsibility and recognition, and what are its promotion channels and salary increase policies?
26. Do employees considered to be promising and steady leave when you least expect it, at a time that is disadvantageous, or at a point in their careers when you feel they should remain with you?
27. What ways do you have of finding out why these people leave?
28. What is done to analyze these situations with a view to preventing them in the future?
29. If such occurrences have been analyzed, comment briefly on the statistical evidence as well as the trends that it suggests.
30. Does the company have written personnel policies or regulations that are available to everyone?
31. Is your product or service market expanding? If so, why? If not, why not?
32. In what ways do you expect your product or service market to change in the next year and the next three to five years?
33. To what major classification of industry does your business belong?
34. What major problems face the industry immediately and in the long range?

35. What reliable sources provided the information you used in answering question 34?
36. What major pieces of legislation in the last 20 years have most significantly affected the way you conduct your business?
37. What discriminatory practices against minorities are condoned in your company?
38. Analyze the employees currently in your business as follows:
    What percentage of your current staff has a master's or doctor's degree?
    What percentage has a bachelor's degree?
    What percentage has some college education?
    What percentage graduated from high school?
    What percentage graduated from elementary school only?
    What is the percentage of black, Chicano, or other minority group members in each job category? What is the percentage of all minority groups in each job category?
    What is the median age of those in management in each job category within the organization?
    What is the percentage of minority group members **in hourly or** nonexempt jobs?
    What percentage of your workforce is considered skilled?
    What percentage is considered semiskilled?
    What percentage is considered unskilled?
    In which of the skilled, semiskilled, and unskilled groups are you experiencing the highest, the second-highest, and the lowest percentage of turnover this year?
    Is this a typical pattern in your business?
    For how many years has this pattern been typical?
    In what specific job titles or kinds of work has the number of employees increased the most in the past year, the past three years, and the past five years?
    In what specific job titles or kinds of work has the number of employees decreased in the periods just cited?
    What jobs are considered pivotal or springboard positions for promotion?
    What jobs are strictly dead ends?
    Of those manning dead-end jobs, how many do you consider good or potentially good employees?
    What is the probability (high, moderate, or low) of their continuing in these dead-end jobs for 6 months, 12 months, or 24 months longer?
39. Assuming that the turnover pattern in your company is unsatisfactory and costly, what has been done to correct it?

40. What tangible efforts have been made to improve the quality of the workforce in terms of employees' usable skills and knowledge applicable to present and future jobs?
41. Describe precisely the part each key manager plays in helping the organization reach its profit or operations objectives or in maintaining successful product or service sales.
42. How many middle and lower managers or assistants presently employed by the organization could one day assume top management responsibility?
43. Analyze this group for average age, education, years of service, and time in present position, and estimate when each person should be ready for significant advancement.
44. Rank the five most important factors, including human resources, contributing to the success of the business.

index

advancement, need for, 134
  see also promotion
age discrimination, 63–65
Age Discrimination Act (1967), 63
age factors, in turnover, 84
antidiscrimination
  active policies in, 55–56
  history of, 51–52
anxiety, job performance and, 13
applicant
  attitude and motivation in, 113
  in employment process, 104–105
  external source of, 106–107
  maturity and judgment in, 113–114
Argyris, Chris, 3
attitude, in employment interview, 113
attitude change, problem of, 27–28
attitude survey, turnover and, 89–90

behavior, needs and, 15–16
behavior changes, learning and, 27
black applicants, hiring of, 58–61
black communities, Civil Rights Act and, 56–57
black employees, performance appraisals for, 62–63
  see also minority employees
Blake, R. R., 3
bonuses and incentives, 7–8
boredom, specialization and, 35–36
breaking-in costs, turnover and, 72–73
Brown v. Board of Education of Topeka, 52
business status inventory, in turnover action program, 152–155

centralized organization, vs. decentralized, 21–25
change
  in attitudes, 27–29
  manager as agent of, 26–27
  motivation theories and, 3–7
  organization vs. department, 26
  resistance to, 25–26
  specialization and, 46–47
Civilian Conservation Corps, 52
civil rights
  government action in, 51–53
  pledges in, 65
Civil Rights Act (1964), 50–52, 63, 109
  business community and, 53–56
  color-blindness and, 54–55
  employment processes and, 53
  minority communities and, 56–57
Civil Service Act, 51
Civil War, U.S., 51
color-blindness, Civil Rights Act and, 54

commitment, in manager, 26–27
communication, specialization and, 41–42
conflict, job performance and, 14
counseling, in turnover problem, 88–89

decentralized organization, 21–25
  job descriptions and procedures in, 24
decision making, in employment process, 115–116
discharges
  cost of, 69
  turnover and, 86
  see also exit interview
discriminatory policies
  civil rights and, 53–54
  hiring practices and, 58–61
  older workers and, 64
dissatisfiers, job environment and, 6
Dobbins v. *Local 212*, 53
doomsday job
  defined, 2–3
  enriching of, 18
doomsday organization
  defined, 20
  renewing of, 19–31

economic motivators, 7–8
education, turnover and, 84
ego needs, 6
Eisenhower, Dwight D., 52
Emancipation Proclamation, 51
employee
  attitude of, 113
  dissatisfaction of, 2
  in exit interview, 93–95
  external sources for recruiting of, 106–107
  guilt feelings in, 94
  motivation of in interview, 113
  referrals of in employment process, 107
  rejected, 122
  termination or discharge of, 69, 83–85, 91–102
  upgrading of, 71

employment barriers, for minority groups, 57–58
employment expenses, turnover and, 72
employment interview, 107–109
employment process
  applicant requirements in, 104–105
  company needs and job requirements in, 104–105
  decision making in, 115–116
  elements in, 114–116
  improvement of, 103–119
  intangible qualifications in, 113–114
  interview in, 107–109
  motivation in, 105
  recruitment methods in, 105–107
  referrals in, 107
  selection practices in, 105, 116–118
  testing in, 109–112
environment change, attitude and, 28
equal employment, pledges in, 65
Equal Employment Opportunity Commission, 50, 52–53, 55
Equal Pay Act (1968), 50, 63
ethnic groups, employment barriers for, 57–58
executive turnover, reasons for, 17–18
exit interview, 91–102
  advantages and disadvantages of, 102
  analysis and interpretation of, 99–102
  conducting of, 96–99
  exiting employee in, 93–95
  interviewer in, 93
  interrogation forms in, 95–96
  open-question techniques in, 97–99
  synthesis of findings in, 101–102
expansion rate, calculation of, 70

Fair Employment Practices Committee, 52

fringe benefits, as motivators, 8
frustration, job performance and, 12–13
functional myopia, specialization and, 40

Grid® (Blake-Mouton), 3

Herzberg, Frederick, 6–7
hiring practices, discrimination in, 58–61
see also employment process

industrial relations manager, turnover and, 137–139
intangible costs, in turnover, 77
intelligence tests, in employment process, 110
interdependence, specialization and, 45–46
internal motivation, 10
interview, *see* employment interview; exit interview
interviewer, role of in exit interview, 93
involvement, renewal and, 30–31

job applicants, source of, 106–107
job bidding, feedback in, 122
job classification, in turnover data, 85
job conditions, employee performance and, 2–3
job content
  for minority employees, 61–63
  motivation and, 10–11
job descriptions, organization and, 23–24
job environment
  improvement of, 10–15
  needs hierarchy and, 5
job participation, motivation through, 9
job performance
  appraisal and criteria in, 123–126
  contradiction and conflict in, 14
  vs. job conditions, 2

  negative environmental influences in, 14–15
  stress and tension in, 11–12
  thwarting and frustration in, 12–13
  uncertainty and anxiety in, 13–14
job satisfaction, turnover and, 16–18
job termination, reasons for, 85–88
  see also discharges; exit interview
Johnson, Lyndon B., 52–53
judgment, in employee candidate, 113–114

Kennedy, John F., 52

Labor Department, U.S., turnover rates of, 84
language, as employment barrier, 58
layoffs, turnover and, 71
leadership, renewal and, 30
learning behavior, change and, 27
Likert, Rensis, 3
Lincoln, Abraham, 51
line manager
  in turnover action program, 145–147
  turnover problem responsibility of, 137–139
linking pin and interaction influences theory, 3
Little Rock, Ark., desegregation at, 52
Lombardi, Vince, 12

management, support of promotion system by, 133–134
manager
  as agent of change, 26–29
  responsibility of in turnover action program, 137–139, 145–149
  span of control of, 41
manpower inventory, in turnover action program, 151–152
manpower planning approach, 151
Maslow, Abraham H., 3, 5–6
mass production
  boredom and, 35–36
  job satisfaction and, 17

Index

maturity, in employee interview, 113–114
McGregor, Douglas, 3–5
minority applicants, performance appraisals for, 62
minority communities, Civil Rights Act and, 56–57
minority employees
  barriers to, 57–58
  hiring of, 58–61
  interview of, 60
  job content for, 61
  waste of, 49–65
mix model, 3
money, as motivator, 7
motivation
  achievement and, 149–150
  in employment process, 105, 113
  internal, 10
  job content and, 10–11
  limitations in, 9–10
  methods of, 7–9
  psychological techniques in, 8–9
  in turnover action program, 149–150
motivation theories, 3–7
motivators, economic, 7–8
Mouton, J. S., 3

National Industrial Recovery Act, 52
needs
  behavior and, 15–16
  cultural differences in, 16
  sensitivity to, 20
needs hierarchy, 3, 5–6

older workers, discrimination against, 64
organization
  centralized vs. decentralized, 21–25
  functional relationships in, 21–22
  job descriptions and, 23–24
  management and supervision in, 22–23
  people orientation and, 24–25
  specialization in, 34–47
  turnover and, 20

organization change, resistance to, 25–26
organization responsiveness, turnover and, 90
organization values, performance criteria and, 124–126

participation, renewal and, 30–31
pay grade, job classification and, 85
pay practices, in turnover, 86, 126–127
  see also money
peer pressure, impact of, 28–29
Pendleton Act (1883), 51
people orientation, organization and, 24–25
performance appraisal, in promotion process, 123–126
performance criteria, organization values and, 124–126
performance objectives, in promotion process, 125
perseverance, specialization and, 36–37
personal aspirations, promotions and, 129–132
Peskin, D. B., 108 n., 152 n.
physiological needs, 5
Plessy v. *Ferguson*, 51
problem solving, in employment process, 114–115
problem-solving network, in turnover action program, 148
production workers, motivation of, 9–10
productivity
  negative environmental influences on, 14–15
  vs. pay, in turnover analysis, 74–75
professionalism, promotions and, 128–129
professional specialization, 37–38
promotion
  perception of, 129–132
  performance objectives in, 125–126
  personal aspirations and, 129–132
  professionalism and, 128–129

salary and, 126–127
turnover and, 86
promotion process
 advancement needs in, 134
 improving of, 121–134
 job categories in, 128–129
 management support and, 133–134
 performance factors in, 123–126
promotion system, limitations on, 132–134
psychological techniques, in motivation, 8–9

questionnaires, in exit interview, 95–96

Ramspeck Act (1940), 52
recruitment methods, 105–107
renewal
 change and, 26–28
 mandate for, 27
 need for, 20–21
 organization and, 22–25
 purpose of, 31
 specialization and, 46–47
 task forces in, 29
 team efforts in, 29–30
Roosevelt, Franklin D., 52
round robin interviewing, 108–109

safety needs, 5
salary
 vs. productivity, 76
 promotion and, 126–127
satisfiers and dissatisfiers, 6–7
scarcity principle, 39–40
second effort, in job performance, 12
selection practices
 aspiration level and, 131–132
 errors in, 116–118
 upgrading of, 119
 see also employment process
self-fulfillment needs, 6
separation expenses, in turnover cost, 73–74
service departments, "fighting back" in, 39–40

sex discrimination, 63–65
sex factors, in turnover, 84–85
short-timer costs, in turnover, 72, 74
social needs, 5
social security tax payments, 74
span of control, 41
specialist
 authority role of, 38
 management of, 40–41
specialist–advisers, 43–45
specialist–employees, 42–43
specialization
 added stress from, 45–46
 boredom and, 35–36
 communication and, 41–42
 functional myopia in, 40
 interdependence and, 45
 organization renewal and, 46–47
 perseverance in, 36–37
 professional, 37–38
 task, 34–37
specialty departments, 38–40
startup costs, turnover and, 73
stress
 job performance and, 11–12
 specialization and, 46
superior–subordinate ratio, 22–23
supervision, organization and, 22–23
Supreme Court, U.S., 51

tangible costs, in turnover, 72–77
task force
 organization of, 142–143
 in renewal process, 29–30
task specialization, 34–37
team efforts, 29–31
 participation and involvement in, 30–31
technical specialization, 33–47
 see also specialization
tension
 job performance and, 11–12
 specialization and, 46
testing
 in employment process, 109–112
 evaluation of against norm, 112
Theory X and Theory Y, 3–5

training costs, turnover and, 73, 76
Truman, Harry S., 52
turnover
   age and sex factors in, 84
   analysis of, 82–83
   approaches in, 81–82
   attitude survey on, 89–90
   breaking-in costs in, 72–73
   causes of, 79–90
   company size and, 82
   companywide analysis of, 69–71
   correlations in, 86–87
   counseling and, 88–89
   data correlation in, 141–142
   department analysis of, 71–72
   education background in, 84
   employment expenses in, 72
   executive, 17–18
   expansion rate and, 70
   job classification and pay grade in, 85
   job satisfaction and, 16–18
   length of service and, 85
   management attention in, 78
   organization change and, 20
   organization complexity and, 82
   organization responsiveness and, 90
   pay vs. productivity in, 74–75
   personal reasons for, 2–3
   separation expenses and, 73–74
   short-timer costs in, 72, 74
   social security tax payments in, 74
   startup costs and, 73
   statistical methods of study in, 69–72
   tangible cost factors in, 72–77
   termination reasons given for, 85–88
   training costs and, 73, 76
   true cost of, 75–77
   unemployment insurance and, 74
turnover action program, 134–150
   business status inventory in, 152–155
   conference on progress in, 145–147
   line management evaluation in, 145–147
   line management organization and activation in, 143–145
   management mandate in, 142
   manpower inventory and planning in, 151–152
   motivation and achievement in, 149–150
   problem-solving network in, 148
   task force organization in, 142
turnover analysis program
   alternate research methods in, 88–90
   analytic and predictive data in, 87–88
   basic information needed in, 83–85
   design of, 82–83
turnover costs
   handling of, 140–141
   intangible, 77
   measurement of, 67–78
   true value of, 75–77
turnover problem
   as manager's job, 139–149
   responsibility for, 137–139
turnover rate, calculation of, 70

uncertainty, job performance and, 13–14
Uncle Tomism, 56
unemployment, of minorities, 61–62
unemployment insurance, turnover and, 74

verbal skill tests, in employment process, 110–111
vocational proficiency tests, 111
Volstead Act (1919), 51

women, discrimination against, 63–64
work milieu, impact of, 10–15

Zimmerer, Thomas, 76